PEDRO PINO

Pedro Pino (Lai-iu-ah-tsai-lu) wearing a native blue wool woven shirt, belt of silver medallions, and shell bead necklace. Photograph by John K. Hillers, probably taken in Washington, D. C., in 1882. National Anthropological Archives, Smithsonian Institution, 2232A.

PEDRO PINO

Governor of Zuni Pueblo, 1830–1878

E. Richard Hart

Foreword by T. J. Ferguson

UTAH STATE UNIVERSITY PRESS
Logan, Utah

Utah State University Press
Logan, Utah 84322-7800

Royalties from the sale of this book will be donated to the Zuni Senior
Center, Pueblo of Zuni.

Cover design by K. C. Muscolino.

Cover photo, foreground: Pedro Pino, photograph by John K. Hillers,
1882 (National Anthropological Archives, Smithsonian Institution,
2232A). Background: The Pueblo of Zuni, photograph by Timothy
O'Sullivan, 1873.

Manufactured in the United States of America

Printed on acid-free paper

Library of Congress Cataloging-in-Publication Data

Hart, E. Richard.
  Pedro Pino : governor of Zuni Pueblo, 1830-1878 / E. Richard Hart ;
foreword by T. J. Ferguson.
      p. cm.
Includes bibliographical references and index.
  ISBN 0-87421-562-5 (hardcover : alk. paper) — ISBN 0-87421-563-3
(pbk. : alk. paper)
  1. Pino, Pedro. 2. Zuni Indians—Kings and rulers—Biography.
3. Governors—New Mexico—Zuni—Biography. 4. Zuni Indians—
History—19th century. 5. Zuni Indians—Government relations.
6. Zuni (N.M.)—History—19th century. 7. Zuni (N.M.)—Politics and
government. I. Title.
  E99.Z9 P554 2003
  978.9'83—dc21
                                    2002156452

Contents

Illustrations

Foreword

This is a remarkable book about a remarkable man. Lai-iu-ah-tsai-lu, also known as Pedro Pino, was the most prominent Zuni political leader of the nineteenth century. Born into the Eagle Clan in 1788, Lai-iu-ah-tsai-lu was captured by the Navajos in his early teens and later sold to Don Pedro Bautista Pino, a prominent citizen in New Mexico. Don Pedro exposed Lai-iu-ah-tsai-lu to Spanish colonial culture and government and became his namesake in subsequent dealings with non-Zuni people.

During his sojourn away from his tribe, Lai-iu-ah-tsai-lu gained invaluable knowledge of the geography and peoples of New Mexico, as well as the political operation of the colonial government that held sway over the Zuni people. His Spanish benefactor eventually returned Lai-iu-ah-tsai-lu to Zuni Pueblo, intending that he continue his education under the tutelage of the Spanish priest at the Catholic mission. After several years, however, Lai-iu-ah-tsai-lu sought refuge in an outlying farming village, staying there until the mission was abandoned in 1821. This village, Heshota, now lies in ruin on the mesa north of Zuni Pueblo. Its silent walls give mute testimony to a bygone era that has largely faded from historical consciousness.

After Lai-iu-ah-tsai-lu returned to Zuni Pueblo, he was initiated into the Priesthood of the Bow, charged with providing spiritual and military protection for the Zuni people. Lai-iu-ah-tsai-lu was also initiated into other esoteric religious societies, including the Kea-shi-kwe, or Cactus Fraternity. He is remembered as a great orator, well versed in Zuni culture and tradition, and a leader of many successful war parties.

Lai-iu-ah-tsai-lu served as the governor of the Pueblo of Zuni during most of the period from 1830–1878. He was multilingual, speaking Zuni, Navajo, and Spanish. His knowledge of Navajo and Spanish culture and government stood him in good stead during the Mexican period between 1821 and 1846 and prepared him to deal with the United States when it asserted political control over the Southwest. Lai-iu-ah-tsai-lu forged alliances with the United States and other Indian nations that helped protect Zuni people from the increasing depredations of neighboring Navajo bands.

During his tenure as governor, Lai-iu-ah-tsai-lu formulated and implemented a foreign policy that steered his tribe through a politically and economically perilous period when Zuni lands were taken by the United States and the Zuni people were forced to adapt to a new American economy and culture. Lai-iu-ah-tsai-lu toiled throughout his life to document the tribe's aboriginal lands and maintain Zuni sovereignty over them.

Promoting trade in Zuni agricultural products and natural resources was one of the means Lai-iu-ah-tsai-lu used to improve economic development in the face of a diminished land base. Lai-iu-ah-tsai-lu combined trade agreements with a political alliance with the United States, and the Zuni tribe thus supplied the United States Army with critical provisions to support Fort Defiance and other military posts in the Southwest. In addition, under Lai-iu-ah-tsai-lu's leadership, the Zuni people also assisted government expeditions and wagon trains of American migrants heading west to California.

The midnineteenth century was a troubling time for Zuni people, who were beset by epidemics of smallpox and other diseases that periodically and tragically reduced the size of the population. The able leadership of Lai-iu-ah-tsai-lu substantially helped to mitigate the dire situation facing the Zuni people during this period.

When he was more than 90 years old, Lai-iu-ah-tsai-lu accompanied a delegation of Zuni leaders to Washington, D.C., where he met the president of the United States and other prominent politicians. During this visit, Lai-iu-ah-tsai-lu climbed to the top of the recently constructed Washington Monument, where he viewed the nation's capital. This trip was instrumental in helping Zuni leaders recognize and assess the cultural habits, political power, and technological achievements of Euro-Americans.

Throughout his career, Lai-iu-ah-tsai-lu's political activities as the Zuni governor were based on statesmanship, diplomacy, defense of sovereignty, honesty, moral authority, patience, hospitality, and friendliness. This political legacy sets a high leadership standard that all contemporary politicians, Zuni and non-Zuni, would do well to emulate.

Much of what we know about Lai-iu-ah-tsai-lu comes from the letters and documents he assiduously collected from the foreigners who passed through Zuni Pueblo. These papers include messages from a cross-section of the notable Americans who traveled through the West, people such as Ives, Whipple, Beale, Wheeler, Cushing, Sherman, Bourke, and Washington. Even though he could not read English, Lai-iu-ah-tsai-lu knew the importance of these documents and carefully maintained an archive for the benefit of his people. Lai-iu-ah-tsai-lu's papers were eventually acquired by the anthropologist Frank Hamilton Cushing. After Cushing's death, his brother-in-law, Frederick Webb Hodge, secreted Cushing's papers in a trunk, including the documents he had obtained from Lai-iu-ah-tsai-lu. These papers were rediscovered after Hodge's death in 1956, and they are now available for study at the Southwest Museum in Los Angeles. Hart makes extensive use of these archival documents in crafting his book about the life and times of Lai-iu-ah-tsai-lu.

Hart successfully accomplishes a difficult task in this book. His scholarly research is meticulous and thorough, but he rises above the dry, lifeless prose of many historical narratives to animate the life and times of Lai-iu-ah-tsai-lu in a vivid style that is readily accessible to the average reader. Furthermore, in much of the published historical and anthropological literature of Zuni, individuals are subsumed under the more general treatment of the tribe as a whole. Hart's book addresses this shortcoming by focusing on Lai-iu-ah-tsai-lu as a person. While there is a genre of autobiographies of Native Americans in the twentieth century, there are fewer biographies of nineteenth-century American Indians, and Hart's work redresses this problem.

In writing the biography of an exceptional Zuni leader, Hart illuminates the social, political, and economic contexts of Zuni history during the eighteenth and nineteenth centuries. While maintaining a penetrating focus on Lai-iu-ah-tsai-lu, the book provides broad insights into the cultural changes that shaped Zuni and southwestern history during the pivotal period when control over the region shifted from Spain to Mexico to the United States. The book provides a fascinating encapsulation of American history in the West, covering issues ranging from mountain men, government expeditions to explore geology and transportation routes, the Civil War, the Navajo Wars, Indian policy, the establishment of Indian reservations, and the activities of early anthropologists—all viewed through the lens of Lai-iu-ah-tsai-lu and Zuni Pueblo.

Hart has produced a book that is valuable to the Zuni people, scholars, and anyone interested in southwestern history and anthropology. He is to be commended for crafting a solid piece of historical research that is also accessible to multiple audiences. All readers will appreciate the clarity of language and lucid expression of ideas. In addition, scholars will find the multitude of footnotes useful in pursuing research about the people and issues dealt with in the biography. The four appendices provide valuable primary material to supplement the narrative.

Hart finished this manuscript in 1979, following a decade of historical research for the Pueblo of Zuni. For many years, it was only available to those resolute scholars who sought out Hart's papers in archives at the pueblo and the University of Utah Marriott Library. During the 1980s and 1990s, Hart's attention turned to additional research for the Pueblo of Zuni. During this period, he led an interdisciplinary team of scholars who studied Zuni history, culture, and environment to provide the evidence used by the pueblo to successfully litigate a series of land claims. We owe thanks to Hart for finally retrieving his manuscript from the archives and submitting it for publication. An afterword written by Hart in 2002 discusses the audience the original manuscript was intended to serve—the youth of Zuni—and helps place the manuscript into the context of contemporary historiographic and political issues. Hart's biography of Lai-iu-ah-tsai-lu stands the test of time and is as rewarding to read today as it was when it was written more than twenty years ago.

In a fitting tribute to Lai-iu-ah-tsai-lu, E. Richard Hart is graciously donating the royalties from the sale of this book to the Zuni Senior Center at the Pueblo of Zuni. This program actively fills the needs of elderly Zuni people, providing them with social activities, companionship, meals, and other support. Thus, more than a century after his life, Lai-iu-ah-tsai-lu continues to serve his people.

T. J. Ferguson
Tucson, Arizona

one
Early Years

Lai-iu-ah-tsai-lu was born into a rich and ancient cultural universe. The proximate environment was and is a relatively hard land, with bitter winters and smoldering summers. It is devastatingly arid; water is worth everything. Yet when it rains, a dry gulch may become a churning river in minutes. He was born into the A:shiwi, or Zuni, tribe, a people who had lived in this particularly tough country for over a millennium, who had lived in their town, or pueblo, on the same spot for five hundred years, making it (with Taos Pueblo, Old Oraibi, and Acoma Pueblo) one of the oldest, continuously occupied communities in the United States. He was born, on his mother's side, into the Eagle Clan, and on his father's side into the Deer Clan. His people are among the most remarkable on this continent, and he was destined to lead them politically through some of their more difficult years.

The Zunis had lived under European rule or influence for two hundred and fifty years when Lai-iu-ah-tsai-lu was born in the last decade of the eighteenth century. Their pueblo was compact and architecturally beautiful, blending artfully with the environment and rising five stories into the air. The people lived in this central pueblo on the Zuni River during the winter, but through the agricultural year spread out as far as the Little Colorado to the west and beyond their Salt Lake to the south. Every available piece of arable land was cultivated. Their trade was vast for the time. Their relations with the government of Spain had been established and tested for many decades by the time Lai-iu-ah-tsai-lu came into the world.

The central village of the Zunis was situated in precisely the same spot where it had been for more than a century, and within a

1

few yards of the place occupied by the people for at least three centuries previous to that.[1] The boundaries of their land had been well fixed at least since the time of Coronado's invasion in 1540.[2] The Zunis were first known to the Spaniards as the people of the "Seven Cities of Cibola." Later, the Zunis' land was referred to as the "Province of Cibola." After the Pueblo Revolt, the central village came to be known as Zuni. Zuni continued to be, as it had been before the Spaniards arrived, a focal point in cultural achievement and a trade center for distant tribes.

Though bilateral Zuni/Spanish expeditions were occasionally necessary to keep the raiding Apaches and Navajos in check, the Zunis traded with both tribes and lived with secure borders under Spanish rule. The Zunis' own government was a theocracy. The *caciques* appointed the secular leaders, including the governor, but they gave him and his *tenientes* much personal discretion. The western pueblos of Zuni, Acoma, and Laguna (after its founding in 1699) were the outposts of the Spanish Empire in North America. In 1790 the Zuni Pueblo was considered by Spaniards to be the last bastion of civilization on the frontier. The tribe joined the Spaniards as auxiliaries, aided military expeditions, and provided many further services.[3] They protected the northern frontiers of the Spanish domain, and in return Spain recognized the Zunis' rights to their aboriginal land holdings. Zuni land was held in common, could not be sold, and was protected meticulously by the Crown. As a Spanish decree of 1811 put it, the pueblos were granted "the right of planting and cultivating all the land which their ability and circumstances permitted them to do so."[4]

Lai-iu-ah-tsai-lu was reportedly an uncommonly bright and strong youth, and at an early age, thirteen or fourteen, was already joining in the retaliatory war parties sent out against the Navajos.[5] For a number of years, it had been necessary for the Zunis to join the Spaniards as allies in these expeditions against the Athabascans. At about the time of Lai-iu-ah-tsai-lu's birth in 1788, 294 Zunis were listed as members of the Spanish army—one captain, one lieutenant, and the remainder privates.[6]

During several campaigns against the Navajos near the close of the century, the raiders were seemingly subdued, and an uneasy peace existed in Zuni country. But as Lai-iu-ah-tsai-lu reached his teens, the fighting again broke out. In 1804–1805 depredations increased to the point that a major attack on the Navajo homeland was planned and carried out. Zunis joined the Spanish command and, in the middle of winter, attacked the Navajos in the heart of their winter territory. Moving against the Navajos from the Zuni base of operations, the allied command of soldiers met the enemy in what came to be known as Canyon del Muerto. More than one hundred men, women, and children were among the Navajo dead, while the Zunis reported that only one of their number, a leader, was killed.[7]

It was at about this time, while young Lai-iu-ah-tsai-lu was out on a war party with his father, his uncle, and others, that he was captured by the Navajos.[8] It must have been a shattering experience to the young man: distinguished in war, only thirteen or fourteen years old, and in the hands of his people's old enemies. Slavery was not uncommon under the Spanish rule. In fact, the Spaniards seemed to encourage it even among their enemies, the Navajos.[9] Thus, it was probably because Lai-iu-ah-tsai-lu was young, strong, and intelligent, and therefore a valuable commodity as a slave, that he was not executed but instead saved to sell to the highest bidder.

He was held in captivity for what must have been an interminable time, perhaps as long as two years, but there were some positive results of his enslavement. During the period, he learned fluent Navajo and much about the habits and discipline of his people's sometimes enemies. Traveling with his captors, he saw the homeland of the Navajos as well as the areas they traversed throughout the year. Undoubtedly he saw raiding parties go out in the spring after the Navajos' planting had been completed, on their way to steal from the Spanish and Pueblo Indian settlements. Then, in the fall, when the Navajos were ready to harvest their corn, Lai-iu-ah-tsai-lu watched the raiding parties return and the Navajos move home to Canyon de Chelly for the winter.

Eventually Lai-iu-ah-tsai-lu was ransomed from his captors by a wealthy Spaniard, one Pedro Pino—likely Don Pedro Bautista Pino, the author of *The Exposicion of Don Pedro Bautista Pino, 1812*.[10] Pedro Pino was one of the most influential Spaniards in Santa Fe during the period, and also one of the wealthiest. When, in 1810, the people of the Nueva Mexico province wanted a representative to visit Spain to plead for more support, it was Pedro Pino who was chosen. He did travel to Spain and in vain tried to reach the king's ears, but eventually, after two years of pleading, he reluctantly gave up and wrote his *Exposicion* before returning home.[11] So the young Zuni, Lai-iu-ah-tsai-lu, was in the care of perhaps the most knowledgeable person in this Spanish territory when it came to politics. And Lai-iu-ah-tsai-lu was evidently also in the care of one who wanted his slave educated.

The young Zuni was still a captive but now he was learning the Spanish system. He not only studied how the New Mexican government worked under the Spaniards, but he actually met the people who held the power and ran the government. He met and spoke with the leaders of the province, who all associated with Pedro Pino. He likely learned the policies which the Spaniards wanted to maintain with the Zunis and the other western pueblos—that they were citizens in some ways, but not in others. The Zunis were allies, and their lands were undeniably their own forever under Spanish law, but they were not permitted to sell or otherwise alienate their own lands. The young Zuni also discovered that the Spanish form of government in the Southwest was almost universally corrupt. Bribery and friendship were the means to get things done, the accepted form of government. Lai-iu-ah-tsai-lu evidently became knowledgeable in the ways of the "diplomats" of the time.

When he was finally returned to his own people, Lai-iu-ah-tsai-lu was a different person. It was not just that he had become a man. He knew the Navajos and their lands and could speak their tongue. He knew about the Spaniards' government and their policies and could speak fluent and indeed eloquent Spanish.

It may have been when Pedro Bautista Pino was appointed to visit Spanish authorities that he decided to return Lai-iu-ah-tsai-lu to his people. Pino evidently intended that the young Zuni's education should not end there. He apparently had high hopes for the young man and to further encourage his advancement, put him in the charge of the Spanish priest at the Zuni Mission. This must have been like a third captivity for Lai-iu-ah-tsai-lu. The priest and the mission were strict. For three or four years, he was forced to endure this harshly disciplined life and continue his European education. As an old man, Lai-iu-ah-tsai-lu would recall that he had been unable to find much worth in this education. As a result, he had rebelled against the priest's hard regimen and escaped to the Zuni village of Heshota, north of the main village, where he probably remained in semiseclusion until Mexican independence in 1821, when the Spaniards abandoned their mission at the pueblo (for some time there had been no resident priest there).[12]

Lai-iu-ah-tsai-lu made a lasting tribute to his former Spanish "father." Throughout the remainder of his life, in all of his dealings with non-Zunis, he took the name of Pedro Pino. Pedro Pino the Zuni would come to be one of the most important men to his people for the next sixty years. All of the adversity of his various captivities had prepared the young man for the future political turmoil he would face. Among his tribe, he was the most knowledgeable about "secular" life outside the pueblo. In 1821, when the mission was abandoned, he was probably one of the few who recognized the potential negative consequences which would accompany the positive results of the priests' departure.

Lai-iu-ah-tsai-lu was able to move back into the main pueblo now that the priests were gone. He had married at the age of seventeen or eighteen and so lived among his wife's family. He would remain with his wife for seventy or more years, living faithfully with her until his death. Living again with his own people, he was able to continue his Zuni religious education. He continued to be active in the military arm of the tribe and was first made a member of a war medicine fraternity and later initiated into the Priesthood of the Bow. He never forsook his military obligations, despite his early enslavements, and eventually became one of the highest office holders in the priesthood. Always active in his people's religion, he would hold several other spiritual positions throughout the remainder of his long career.

Pedro Pino the Zuni likely knew why the Spaniards valued the Zunis' alliance and territory. When asked why the Zuni territory was so important to the Spaniards, he could explain that it constituted what the Spaniards believed was a route to the Pacific Ocean. Ever since the Pueblo Revolt of 1680, the Spaniards had conjectured that this possibility existed, and thus the western pueblos had often received somewhat better treatment. It was not just because appropriations from the crown depended on the territory administered by the province, nor because of the relatively long distance between Santa Fe and the pueblos of Zuni, Acoma, and Laguna, but also because this valuable corridor had to be protected and the Spaniards could not do it by themselves. They were forced to treat the western pueblos, and especially the Zunis, as allies. San Diego was founded in 1769 and Monterey in 1770. After the Dominguez-Escalante expedition established the possibility of a Spanish Trail to California, Spanish authorities supplied Zuni with arms and ammunition and went on joint expeditions to protect not only the Zunis' land but the territory which they hoped would someday provide the province with an overland route connecting their California settlements to New Mexico.

If Pino had learned this much from his namesake, he probably also deduced the potential meaning when, on September 27, 1821, Mexico gained her independence from Spain, and New Mexico became a province of the new republic. Many of the villages of Mexicans celebrated independence with a small fiesta, but to most of the inhabitants of New Mexico, Indian and Mexican alike, independence made little difference in their daily lives. Pino may have known from his namesake that trade between the United States and Mexico was beginning to open up and that goods and people were starting to flow across the Santa Fe Trail. This movement was in part responsible for the sudden new presence of American fur trappers in Zuni territory. And young Pedro may have suggested that, since the mission was now abandoned and Mexico was independent, closer ties with the government in Santa Fe would be necessary. The alliance must be kept.

Pedro Pino's people in the period numbered perhaps three thousand inhabitants, most of whom lived in the central village of Halona:wa. They raised extensive corn and wheat crops in fields spread over an area from present-day St. Johns, Arizona, to the Zuni Mountains in what is now western New Mexico. Their herds of more than fifteen thousand sheep grazed across an area from the Little Colorado to the Zunis' Salt Lake and beyond. The potential enemies of the Zunis were across the Rio Puerco (the Navajos) and south beyond the Zuni Salt Lake in the mountains (Apaches—from a Zuni word meaning "enemy").

Zuni country has an ageless quality, and each season illuminates it from a new, scrutinizing perspective. With the hard winters, hot and dry summers, and magnificent desert spring and fall seasons, there was good hunting for bear, deer, elk, and other big game in each of the four directions. All of the land in the province of Zuni was used by the people, whether for practical or spiritual preservation. The Ashiwi knew which clay lay in which strata in a mesa to the south and that it was best for a certain type of pottery. They knew that a specific herb along the Little Colorado (in what is now Arizona) would treat a certain malady. They knew that they had grazed their sheep (acquired from the Spaniards) near the base of the Zuni Mountains for centuries.[13]

Most importantly, the Ashiwi knew the boundaries of their land. No one person owned a plot here and another there (although clans held hereditary use rights). The people held the land communally. No one could sell a piece of what belonged to all. The boundaries were specific: in the northeast, Mount Taylor provided the boundary point of Zuni territory; to the east, lava beds formed a natural barrier between the people of Zuni and the Ha-ku-we (people of Acoma);[14] to the south, after the conquest of the Keresan pueblos of Marata around 1540,[15] the mountains encircling the valleys around the Zuni Salt Lake and Rito Quemado created the boundary; to the southwest and west, the Little Colorado formed another natural barrier between the Zunis and the Western Apaches (who habitually raided Zuni nevertheless); the A'muk wikwi or Hopis were to the northwest, and a division line between them and the Ashiwi existed near Pueblo Colorado Wash; to the north, the marauding bands of Navajos did not venture to settle farther south than a longitudinal line which would run (approximately) through the present-day town of Gallup, New Mexico and extend westward to Twin Buttes, the boundary of the A'muk wikwi (Hopis).[16]

The Zunis had been secure under Spanish rule. The Province of Cíbola boundaries had been rigid and acknowledged by the government.[17] Now it appeared that things might get better still. The people were free of the priests and thus able to practice their own religion unhampered by the Catholic Church's manipulations. They had always been a trading people and, with the opening of the Santa Fe Trail bringing Americans into their territory, their commerce would increase.

The newfound freedom of religion was extremely important to the Zunis. Religion permeated their existence. The land was their church. Practically every spring of water in the area was visited periodically for purely ceremonial purposes. Kothluwalawa (Kolhu/wala:wa), the sacred lake in Arizona, is one of the most, if not the most, spiritual spots to the people of Zuni Pueblo.[18] There and at the Zuni Salt Lake to the south many important ceremonials were performed throughout the year. The Zunis' life was filled with ceremony, with beauty in ritual, symbol, and metaphor. Theirs was the "Middle Place," not only the center of the six directions— east, west, north, south, zenith, and nadir—but also a metaphorical middle or moderate lifestyle. A person's "road" was his or her life. It might be a rough or an easy road, but one should never worry about the eventual destination. "Worry is the most serious of all illnesses; it is the sickness of the spirit."[19] Prayers for another person include the plea, "May their roads come in safely."[20]

The Zunis' origin story is one of the classic pieces of religious poetry in existence. Many have translated and written of it.[21] The story begins, "Laying their lightning arrow across their rainbow bow, they drew it. Drawing it and shooting down, they entered."[22] When the Zunis finally came into the light, they exclaimed, "Oh, Dear! Is this what we look like?"[23] The remarkable description of their human appearance in the first light of day includes "slimy tails, slime-covered bodies, and webbed fingers."[24] The Zuni culture spans a period equal to that encompassed by our scientific appraisal of the human condition.

The humility of the people of Zuni is represented in the prayer of the bow priest in summer retreat:

All my ladder descending Children
All of them I hold in my hands . . .
Those yonder in the east,
In all the villages that stand against the place of the rising sun,
Even to all those villages
That stand against the place of the setting sun,
Even every little bug,

Even every dirty little bug,
Let me hold them all fast in my hands
Let none of them fall from my grasp—
In order that this may be,
My fathers,
I ask you for life.[25]

To the Zunis, the road of life was a serious matter. Crossing another's path involved a commitment to that person. "Here where I live happily you have passed me on my road."[26] People's fates intersected and interconnected: "Sit down. Now speak. I think there is something to say. It will not be too long a talk."[27] There was a commitment to all other life in the Zuni system, and death came "when the heart wears out,"[28] after old age and "snow upon their heads,/With moss upon their faces,/With bony knees,/ no longer upright but bent over canes."[29]

This was Pedro Pino's world. It was a world in which the idea of suicide was so remote and unknown that when it was first mentioned by Europeans, the Zunis laughed.[30] It was a world in which many things taken for granted in our culture were taboo. "Initiative, ambitions, an uncompromising sense of honor and justice, intense personal loyalties—not only are not admired but are heartily deplored."[31] Compromise was necessary to peace. Ambition does not fit in a truly communal society. Chauvinism and egocentrism were frowned upon. Either men or women could take the initiative necessary for courtship.[32] The terms "rich" and "poor" in Zuni poetry do not refer to physical possessions but to the spiritual attributes of an individual. A rich man was a spiritually secure one, and a poor man was spiritually insecure.[33]

Zuni poetry and art demonstrate how the lifestyle survived. Secular affairs were left out of poetry and ceremony. In a way there was a separation of church and state. For instance, there were no ceremonies whatsoever at marriage.[34] Social contracts were not a part of Zuni religion. Love was respected in poetry and ceremony, but "the priests do not act in secular affairs, being too sacred to contaminate themselves with dispute or wrangling."[35]

Each person's place in Zuni society developed slowly, over the years; each individual was unique, so that no one was uneasy about his or her social station.[36] The word for life in Zuni is literally "day-light." "Violence [was] culturally taboo in Zuni."[37] Their lifestyle and culture were that simple and that complex.

It is not, then, unusual that the Zunis were famous through-out the land for their hospitality. For generations writers have spoken of the people's kindness and generosity. These traits were shown to the first Americans who came into the area. Perhaps Pino had told his people stories he had heard in Santa Fe of the Americans' much-heralded wealth. More likely the first Americans were treated just like all visitors. In any case, when the first fur trappers came to Zuni land in the 1820s, passing through the country to trap beaver in the mountains, they were met with unex-pected friendship.

The only road to the trappers' frontier in the Southwest led through Zuni. Here the trappers traded and outfitted themselves to go into regions as yet unexplored by the Anglos. Indeed, the last place where trappers could outfit themselves before entering the "wilderness" was Zuni Pueblo.[38] To trap in these parts of the country, Americans were ostensibly required by the Mexican gov-ernment to obtain a license from the authorities, but in California and the Southwest, many Americans slipped easily in and out with-out consulting the authorities. The Zunis helped those parties that came through their area. By welcoming the Americans, the Ashiwi not only honored their traditions of friendship and respect but improved their material position as well, for the Americans were able to generate more trade goods and thus made trading a more profitable experience for both parties.

One of these early trappers was William Sherley "Old Bill" Williams, who in 1826 was illegally trapping beaver in Apache country, north of the Gila River. Trapping alone one day, he was captured in this remote country by a band of Apaches, who relieved him of everything he owned—his clothes, his weapons, his stock, supplies, and traps.

"Stark naked, afoot, and without a weapon," he headed north-east toward Taos. After a 160-mile travail through the White Mountains, the arid valley of the Little Colorado (the boundary of Zuni territory), and then across the stream and into the desolate country beyond, he was finally found wandering among the dry mesas by a party of Zunis. He was transported to the pueblo, "ceremoniously welcomed, provided with a blanket and moccasins, and 'treated with great veneration . . . .'"39

Old Bill continued to pass through the Zuni country for the next few years, and later became the first American to set eyes on the Zuni Salt Lake. Trapping on the periphery of the Zunis' land, in the Datil Mountains, Williams chanced to pass through the lava beds bordering Zuni land. Topping an ordinary-seeming rise, he came in full view of the marvelous lake with its craters and fields of salt. The fabled lake had been known to the Spaniards since their arrival in 1540, when Coronado came across it after conquering the Zuni pueblo of Hawikku. Coronado had reported with some surprise that in the village there was "salt, the best and whitest I have seen in all my life," and that it had been brought from a "lake a day's journey distant."40

Old Bill looked down on a beautiful volcanic lake hidden in a desert crater and fed by underground saline springs. In the middle of the waters rose up imposing black cinder cones, and around the edges of the lake were flats of pure salt, which was, as the Spaniards had said, of the purest quality. He must also have seen that, stuck in the ground around the lake in the salt flats, were many prayer feathers, or sticks with various colorful feathers tied to them. These were offered in prayer by the Zunis when salt was gathered.

Pedro Pino was likely among some of the groups of Zunis who journeyed to the lake once a year to gather salt for domestic use and trade. The lake had long made Zuni important as a trade center. A fair number of other tribes were allowed by the Zunis to gather salt at the lake, including Acoma, Laguna, the White Mountain Apache, the Cibicue Apache, and some Navajos, but "in recognition of the ownership of the Zunis in this lake, other Indian tribes who [gathered] salt there have always paid them toll for the privilege, and the lake has been a considerable source of revenue for them."41

Old Bill Williams always spoke highly of the Zunis and their marvelous country, but there were few beaver in the area. By 1830 what beaver had been in the mountain streams were so depleted that the fur trappers moved on to other horizons. Perhaps Pino and the Zunis felt some small affinity for the traders, for the Zunis were themselves hunters. They regularly hunted bear, deer, elk, moose, groundhogs, antelope, rabbits and many game birds. Bear were important in the stories of the people, and deer were one of the most important sources for motifs on their strikingly beautiful pottery.[42] In earlier times, the Zunis had hunted buffalo and traded the skins for shells and other items from Indians as far away as present-day Sonora.

Pedro Pino must have participated in the large communal rabbit drives which took place near the summer farming village of Ojo Caliente. He would have used a throwing stick, or boomerang, to bring down not only rabbits but coyotes and other small game. The rabbit sticks were hand carved and often quite elaborate.[43] Another method of communal hunting was described by John G. Owens, who, writing in 1891, said, "I saw a fence about fifteen miles to the southeast of Zuni which, I was told, extended for seventy-five miles, and was formerly used to direct the herds of antelope to a certain spot."[44]

Pino probably also went out once a year to gather the pine nuts from the pinyon trees in the Zuni Mountains. The nuts from these trees were such an important resource to the Zunis that apparently their theft from the Zuni Mountains by Navajos precipitated a war.[45] In other parts of the West, notably Nevada, when whites arrived, they indiscriminately destroyed pinyon forests, thus annihilating the staple of the native peoples and initiating conflicts and wars.

two
First Years as Governor

The Zuni Indians' land was their church, their cathedral. A sharp-faced butte was an altar.[46] A lake was their home in the afterlife, a mesa their hope for this life. The boundaries of their land in 1830 had been relatively exact and intact for hundreds of years. Though threatened by the Navajos and Apaches and ruled to some extent, first by the Spaniards and now by the Mexicans, the Zunis had managed to deal with all invaders. Whether by technology, statesmanship, organization, or defensive military prowess, they had been able to overcome every threat to their existence.

Their complex, well-evolved culture was in large part responsible for this success. Theirs was a true economic equality, and a pervasive cultural equality united the people. Their theocracy worked well in the vast, arid, sparsely populated Nueva Mexico landscape.

Zuni traditional society was organized around the clans, controlled by matriarchs in the intertwined community. The clans held use rights to land and rights to most physical property. The Zunis were governed politically by a theocratic Council of Priests. The bow priests were the executive branch that directly interacted with the secular leaders. Beginning in the Spanish period and persisting through the United States territorial era, Zuni priests were referred to as *caciques*. Civil authorities at Zuni adopted titles from Spanish organization: for instance, governor, lieutenant governor, and *teniente*. These leaders were the equivalents of the tribal chair or chief in other tribes. The *caciques* of the pueblo appointed all the secular leaders, including the governor, who was the central

13

authority on all political matters. Pino's experience with the Navajos, the Mexicans, and the Spanish priests, plus his knowledge of their languages and politics, made him a natural choice as the new governor about 1830.[47]

Pino would remain in office for nearly forty-five years. There were several breaks in his tenure, but they were few and very brief. Though the *caciques* appointed the governor, they were reported to say, "Though it is our place to elect your Governor, it is not for us to say anything that may influence his judgement."[48] In fact, it was considered a very serious breach of policy for a *cacique* as a religious leader to dirty his hands with secular affairs. Pino had much of the weight of the future of the tribe resting on his shoulders for four-and-a-half decades.

During Pino's early years as governor, the tribe's most important occupation was agriculture, as it had been for centuries and would continue to be throughout the nineteenth century. The Zunis practiced a unique form of agriculture in their dry landscape. Utilizing every drop of moisture throughout their expansive area, they implemented floodwater irrigation to nourish their crops. Brush dams were constructed in the washes, where water flowed during the occasional storm, so that silt would deposit behind the dams. By planting in these silted areas, they not only made use of all the available arable land and all the water but at the same time discouraged erosion. (The major gullying in the area began between 1880 and 1910, after territorial pressures caused overgrazing, lumber companies overcut the timber in the Zuni Mountain watershed, and the United States constructed dams that damaged the watersheds.) Crops grew all over the territory of the Zunis, and the people lived in the summers in widely separated villages.

In many ways, this was a rich country. The Zunis were completely self-sufficient and had much produce left over to trade with other tribes and non-Native Americans in the region. "A trade route from Zuni and the Arizona pueblos to the west coast of Mexico was well established by the end of the ninth century."[49] Yet somehow many United States officials persist to this day in their view that the land is "poor" or "worthless."

The Zunis under Pino were strong when threatened. Defensive action was usually undertaken promptly against those who attempted to rob the tribe; the Zunis were competent at controlling their land and carrying out the necessary military actions against those who threatened the peace. But above all, this people was religious. Everything was done with the ceremony of a thoughtful, devout people. They were in touch with their environment and their universe and treated all their crops, their game, their land, and their ceremonial heritage with respect. Theirs was not a Sunday religion but one that encompassed their whole lives and way of life. Their peace and friendliness were noted across the continent and even overseas during the nineteenth century. However, neither European governments nor the later U.S. territorial government ran on the same kind of moral principles as did the Zunis. The governor of Zuni (in Zuni, *tapupu*) had a heavy responsibility. His job was to deal with the interlopers, the thieves, the politicians, and the schemers.[50]

During the 1830s, in his early years as governor, Pedro Pino helped his people expand their jewelry and blacksmith industries. Goods produced by these industries were traded widely to other tribes in the Southwest.[51] This increase in trade helped solidify the tribe's economic status in the Southwest. The Mexican government was not as strong as the Spanish government had been, and trade helped encourage peace in the area. The Zunis were relying more on their own resources to defend their land, though the Mexican government was probably supplying arms and ammunition.

During the decade of the thirties, Pino not only enhanced the position of his tribe through increased trade but also promoted the Zunis' position with the New Mexican government. During the closing years of Mexican rule over New Mexico and Pueblo Indian lands, Pino traveled to Santa Fe, where he was well acquainted and visited often with the last Mexican governor of the territory, Manuel Armijo. At the same time, he was enhancing his position in clan and religious orders.[52] He was respected among the other pueblos and, because of his facility with the Spanish language, was considered influential among the Mexican authorities in Santa Fe.

Under Mexican rule, Indians became quasi-citizens. They were equal in many ways but still did not have the right to alienate their lands.[53] As pressure increased on the New Mexican government from the United States during the closing years of Mexico's domination over the territory, 1841–1846, the territorial government, under Armijo, began to issue more and more land grants.[54] These grants were written for several purposes, a primary one being to encourage the protection of the outer perimeters of New Mexico territory from encroachment by warring Indian tribes and the Americans. It is likely that Pino got some kind of confirmation from the Mexican government for Zuni lands during this period, and, indeed, he later said that he had received a land grant.

Later, after the Americans arrived, the United States made no serious effort to determine Zuni tribal boundaries under Spanish law, but some United States officials did make observations which provided important evidence of Zuni boundaries. George M. Wheeler of the United States Geological Survey described the boundaries as "the following area: Bounded on the north by the dividing ridge between Zuni River and the Puerco, on the east by the summit of the Zuni Mountains, on the south by an east and west line through the Salt Lake, and on the west by the Little Colorado."[55]

Zuni Governor Pino early recognized the value of documents, though he was unable to read and relied on his memory for the content of the papers.[56] Throughout the years he was governor, he tried to retain all the papers written to him that he believed had a relevance to tribal well-being or recorded tribal business transactions. Though the papers were lost or taken from the pueblo in later years, many of them did survive to form an important source of archival material documenting nearly fifty years of Zuni Pueblo history.[57] Without these papers and Pedro Pino's testimony in other documents, much knowledge of the history of Zuni throughout the nineteenth century would surely have been lost.

Other forces were at work in the Nuevo Mexico territory during the period. The pro-Americans, who wanted a government that truly separated church and state, were against the issuance of grants and for a "free" system of government. Thus, since many of the pueblos seemed to be pro-American (Zuni was one) but nevertheless needed their lands confirmed under any government, they found themselves in a political vise. Pino was probably in favor of United States rule but was, on the other hand of course, against the alienation of his people's lands. This conflict would later cause a minor revolt against the U.S. territorial government at the Taos Pueblo. For Zuni it meant that Pino's administration was to become much more complex and difficult.

Governor Pino engaged in trading on behalf of the tribe and knew the important New Mexican merchants. One of these merchants, Juan Cristobal Armijo, who was also pro-American in his political leanings, traded with Zuni under Pino's guidance.[58] Juan Armijo later loaned the United States territorial legislature ten thousand dollars to meet governmental expenses and was one of the more influential New Mexicans throughout the U. S. territorial period.[59]

Throughout the Mexican period, the Zunis remained an outpost on Mexico's frontier, trading their jewelry, blacksmith wares, and blankets with other tribes and protecting their borders against marauders. Although Zuni was relatively secure on the boundaries of Mexico's frontier, there was little doubt in the New Mexico territory as to the outcome of the U.S. war with Mexico. Though there was fighting in Texas and Mexico, enough of the New Mexican leaders were pro-American that there was little resistance when Brigadier general Stephen Watts Kearny's Army of the West entered the Southwest in spite of the fact that the Mexican forces in New Mexico far outnumbered Kearny's troops. The leaders of New Mexico, especially Governor Manuel Armijo, capitulated with barely a battle, following a few brief skirmishes. It was reported that Pino graciously welcomed the conquering American forces when they reached the Zuni Pueblo and was therefore viewed with respect by the American officials.[60] It is evidence of Pino's political acumen that he correctly judged the outcome of the Mexican War from his distant vantage point at Zuni.

Kearny had orders to retain as much of the Mexican government as possible to facilitate the takeover of the territory, but he actually only kept the administrators who were pro-American, a very small minority.[61] Though Pino had known these pro-Americans and dealt with them for years, there is little evidence that they offered any assistance to Zuni under the new American regime.

The archivist for the Armijo administration, Donaciano Vigil, was one of those who stayed on under the United States territorial administration. Vigil certainly knew of the Zunis' land confirmation and the disposition of all pueblo holdings under Mexican and the previous Spanish administrations, but many documents from the period were lost, destroyed, or secreted away. Perhaps we will never know for certain whose responsibility all of the new problems with Pueblo Indian lands were. There are indications that people closely associated with the new administration were involved in land-grant forgeries and deceits even early on.

Navajo raids had continued unabated and, in fact, with increased ferocity as United States troops occupied the territory. Horses, cattle, and thousands of sheep were being stolen from the Mexicans, Pueblo Indians, and other citizens. Shepherds were killed; women and children were kidnaped. To be sure, the Navajos felt some casualties themselves, some of them unprovoked. These drove the raiders to further lengths in their depredations. The people of the outlying pueblo of Zuni had to keep a constant vigil to prevent attacks from Navajos and renegade Mexican Americans alike. When travel was necessary, which was daily, it was done in groups.

By October 5, 1846, the situation was deemed serious enough that Kearny authorized the inhabitants of New Mexico, both Mexican American and Pueblo Indian, to form independent war parties against the Navajos.[62] The next day Colonel Alexander W. Doniphan was authorized to make an excursion into Navajo country and attempt to negotiate a peace treaty with the tribe.[63] During the next five years, four treaties and agreements were signed at Zuni by Governor Pino in an attempt to make peace with the Navajos, but each in turn was broken by the Navajos, usually within a matter of months or even days.

Preliminary to Doniphan's journey into Navajo country, on October 20, Captain John W. Reid left with thirty men to make a reconnaissance of the area west of the Chuska Mountains.[64] As Reid camped on the east side of the Zuni Mountains after talking to some Navajo leaders, a Zuni approached to meet with the officers. The Zuni reported that he had been sent to represent his people, so in all likelihood he was Pedro Pino. A member of Reid's expedition reported that the Zuni had come "to invite us to come and see their women and children: he told us that on his side of the mountain [Zuni Mountains] they were very honest; that three of his children had been taken prisoners by Mexicans and much stock stolen, but if he could obtain his children, he would be satisfied; and they had never yet made war against the Mexicans, and never should. Captain Reid advised him to go to Santa Fe and see the governor."[65]

After concluding a treaty with the Navajos, Doniphan's main command moved on to Zuni, where he hoped to settle upon a peace plan between the two tribes. Doniphan took three Navajo leaders (Zarcillos Largos and Narbona were probably two of them) along with his contingent of troops.[66] The chronicler of this expedition, who evidently had a better interpreter for the Navajo language than for Zuni, reported that the Zunis housed the command and the Navajo visitors in "a spacious adobe building in the city,"[67] and then the negotiations began. The Navajos boasted of being more successful at war than the Zunis and grandly blamed all of the troubles on them, charging that Zunis had killed forty Navajo women who were gathering pine nuts in the Zuni Mountains. A Zuni leader indignantly denied the charge and threatened to hold the Navajos hostage until Zuni captives were released.[68]

The council to arrange a treaty was held on November 26, 1846, and the description of that council is brief. "They met accordingly, and after much debate, consummated a treaty of peace and amity, on the 26th, just and honorable to both parties. This was the last treaty Col. Doniphan made with any tribe of Indians. His labors with the Indians were now finished."[69] The treaty was reported to have given the Zunis the right to govern themselves,[70] for which Pino must have argued strenuously. But neither was the treaty ratified or even submitted to Congress, nor is there a surviving copy of the text. The chronicler of this expedition, like so many who followed him, ended by praising the Zunis for their hospitality. Although the treaty had little effect on the status of the war in the area, it did provide the United States military with a knowledge of a small portion of the Navajo country. By February of 1847, the Navajos had resumed predatory raids in the region.[71]

In September 1847, Major Robert Walker led an expedition against the Navajos. The command passed through Zuni and went on toward the north. But the campaign was poorly planned, and the troops verged on starvation before the Zunis came to the rescue by sending provisions.[72] It was an early example of Pino's and the Zunis' commitment to an alliance with the United States. Although there is no mention in available documents of the Zunis actually joining the United States forces during this period, Cushing later reported that "during the war of the United States with Mexico, the Zunis joined against the Spanish American dominion."[73] Perhaps he was referring to these support services given to the early army expeditions.

In 1848 the Treaty of Guadalupe Hidalgo was signed, officially ending the Mexican War and making New Mexico part of the United States. It also guaranteed that the Pueblo Indians' land would remain forever theirs, as it had been under Spanish and Mexican rule. The situation between the Navajos and both Indian and Hispanic settlements had deteriorated to the point where it was again considered necessary to send a military expedition into Navajo country and attempt another peace negotiation. As with the 1846 expedition, the policy included a stop at Zuni, where a treaty was signed as well as in Navajo country.

Colonel Edward W. B. Newby, commander of the military forces of New Mexico, met with the Navajos on May 20 of that year and signed a treaty with them. It required them to return stolen stock, release all prisoners, and pay for some of their recent depredations.[74] Like all parties dealing with the Navajos during this early territorial period, the army officers did not realize that there was no central leadership within the Navajo tribe. When a few Navajo headmen in one locale or another signed an agreement, it was likely that the vast majority of the tribe in other bands neither heard about the treaty nor felt any obligation to abide by it if they did hear. Some Navajo bands were living in peace with Hispanic and Pueblo Indian settlements, but those bands that were engaging in raids were not likely to change their habits at this point in history without real military pressure, and there was none since the Americans had arrived.

Two of the signers of this May 20 agreement were Pablo Pino and Chapetone.[75] It may be that these names constitute a coincidence—other than the names, there is no evidence that the two were Zunis—but on July 1, empowered by Newby, Colonel Henderson P. Boyakin was at Zuni, where he negotiated another treaty with Governor Pedro Pino and Antonio Chapeton, "Commander of the War Parties of Zuni." Boyakin's orders indicate that he was sent to impress upon the Zunis the fact that the Navajos had signed a treaty with the government and the Zunis were thus obliged to end their war. Evidently the Navajos had made the same allegations against the Zunis because the troops were sent to prevent depredations on the Navajos by the Pueblo Indians, an ironic note at the least. The orders stated that

> the said town of Zuni shall immideatly [*sic*] Comply in Every particular with said treaty on their part, and that they shall from and after this Cease from mistreating said Navajo Indians . . . . The undersigned [Boyakin] further notified said Pueblo de Zuni and its inhabitants that in Case of a Refusal on their part to comply with the provisions of said Treaty Between the Navajo Indians and the United States and in Case they refuse to obey the laws of the United States and New Mexico and the orders of the Commanding officer at Santa Fe then they will be treated as Enemeies [*sic*] of the United States and Troops in Sufficient Numbers will be immideatly [*sic*] marched against This Town to punish them for this refusal.[76]

But Pedro Pino, governor of the Zunis, must have done some fine negotiating during the conference with Boyakin because the agreement signed at Zuni had a somewhat different flavor. The Zunis had been subject to severe restrictions, or attempted restrictions, on their practice of religion under the Spanish government. Pino's foremost considerations must have been to obtain freedom of religion. The U.S. government was promising, in essence, that it would henceforth take care of the peace. The Zunis needn't worry about maintaining an army—the United States was all powerful, and it would take care of the Navajo problem. After the bargaining, Pino and Boyakin signed an agreement which did guarantee that the "Pueblo of Zuni shall Be Protected in the full management of all its rights of private Property and Religion. By the Authorities Civil and Military of New Mexico and the United States." It goes on to state that the Zunis shall obey all United States and New Mexico territorial laws and that the Pueblo of Zuni and the Territory of New Mexico shall "Remain good friends forever[,] that they will always act towards Each other as Brothers."[77]

The words in this agreement typify Pino's relationship with the U.S. for the next thirty years. But the treaty was not even submitted to Congress. Likely the troops did not even keep a copy of the document. Pino and the Zunis were the only ones who remembered the wording. Pino carefully saved his copy of the document for the next three decades.

This agreement made little more difference than the 1846 treaty. That same year a large force of Navajos attacked Zuni. First a Navajo war party diverted the Pueblo warrior defenses to a battle at Pescado, one of the outlying Zuni farming villages; then a larger force attacked the women left at the pueblo from the other direction, the trail to the Hopi villages. "But . . . the women and children successfully defended their homes until the return of the men at night."[78]

During this period, whenever the U.S. sent expeditions against the Navajos, Governor Pino and the Zunis were approached and asked for guides, food, and sometimes additional troops. Food and materials in large quantities were often supplied to the army when it pressed against the Navajos. But the Zunis remembered their promise to refrain from taking action against the Navajos themselves. Cushing commented that "when General Kearny and his successors were, after the Treaty of Guadalupe, subduing the, until then, implacable Navajos the Zunis did invaluable service on our side."[79] This is a considerable understatement.

The war with the Navajos continued unabated, and by September 1849, territorial Governor John M. Washington, Indian Agent James S. Calhoun, and Major H. L. Kendrick left Santa Fe on another expedition to the Navajos. On September 9, 1849, a treaty was signed between Washington and two relatively unimportant Navajo leaders, which, like those before it, required that the Navajos release all of the captive slaves they had in their possession.[80] The party then traveled on to Zuni.

The Navajos were concerned only with getting United States troops out of their homeland. They quickly signed the agreement and then falsely informed the command that they had just received word that Apaches were in the process of attacking Zuni Pueblo. Washington marched his troops to the pueblo and, when he arrived, found that the story about the Apaches was untrue. He learned, in fact, that Navajos had just attempted an attack on the pueblo. The evidence of the recent battle was very apparent. Within a half mile of the village, the body of a Navajo lay in a field. Agent Calhoun reported, "The inhabitants of this Pueblo gave us a hearty reception, manifesting their gratification in the most uproarious, wild and indescribable manner, offering to us large quantities of fruit and bread; all of which was becomingly received."[81] The Zunis made several kinds of bread in their "bee-hive" ovens and raised fruit in their orchards at Dowa Yalanne and Twin Buttes.

Pino met with Governor Washington on several occasions, discussing policy and the situation in the Zunis' part of the country. One of the members of the expedition, James H. Simpson, described the Zuni governor: "A very interesting man we found him to be—about six feet high, athletic in structure, uncommonly graceful and energetic in action, fluent in language, and intelligent—in fact he actually charmed me with his elocution."[82]

The actions of another member of the military detachment may not have seemed quite so charming to the Zunis. Richard H. Kern mentioned in his diary that he "procured" the head of the Navajo lying in the vicinity.[83] Kern was an artist and topographer, who also provided ethnographic information to the army. He had been asked to acquire a head for scientific purposes.

Governor Pino's conversations with Governor Washington led to a transaction in which the Zunis sold the army a supply of corn.[84] Like the Spanish and Mexican armies, the American forces would not have been able to survive in their new western frontier without the Zunis' supplies of corn during the next ten years. Other Americans were quick to take advantage of the Zunis' willingness to deal with U.S. authorities. Agent Calhoun was outraged to learn a short while later that an emigrant train had arrived at Zuni about this time, claiming to be emissaries of the government, and commandeered food, horses, and mules for their trip to California.[85] In these early years of U.S./Zuni contact,

Pino probably had a good deal of trouble determining who really represented the United States government. The problem would only multiply in the years to come.

Under Mexican rule, there had been no effective courts, lawyers, or judges. Justice had been a somewhat whimsical thing, sometimes accomplished mainly through bribes and contacts with powerful New Mexican families. Pino had known some of these families and influential people, and through these contacts the tribe had managed to maintain a remarkably coherent policy with Spain and Mexico, though the government had sometimes seemed arbitrary and occasionally near anarchy. It was no wonder that Pedro Pino had difficulty in identifying the United States government's representatives.

The early territorial courts did not remedy the problems. They were also subject to bribery and corruption, even to the extent that there was a virtual lawless dictatorship by a few leading New Mexico citizens later on. Non-Indian New Mexicans came to the Zuni Pueblo and demanded bribes (usually for fictitious services) when a court decided in favor of the tribe. If the Zunis were lucky enough to win a case in a territorial court—for instance, involving rustling from tribal herds—normally the court costs were higher than the original loss of stock.

By October 1849, the uselessness of the last Navajo/United States treaty had already become apparent to the Zunis. In fact, the treaty had not had the slightest effect on the war situation. Pino and the "captain de guerre" traveled a difficult, two-hundred-mile-long trail to Santa Fe to talk with Indian Agent Calhoun. The United States assurance of protection had amounted to little, according to Pino. Calhoun reported, in a highly revealing letter, some of the difficulties facing the Zuni people:

> The Governor, the Grand Captain and the Captain of War, from Zuni, an Indian Pueblo, which you will remember is two hundred and one 7/100 miles west of Santa Fe, has [*sic*] been with me today.
>
> These are intelligent, active, and athletic Indians, and stated their grievances with great energy, and were especially vehement and vindictive in their denunciations of the faithlessness of all Navajos—they represented they had been greatly harassed

since we left their village on the 16th of September last—that wheresoever they went, they were under the necessity of going guarded and armed, and that they had to watch their horses, mules, and sheep during every hour of the twenty-four. These people asked for arms and ammunition, and permission to make a war of extermination against the Navajos. The deputation from Zuni, also stated there were five-hundred and fifty-five able-bodied men in their village, and only thirty-two fire arms, and less than twenty rounds each for said arms. They spoke confidently of their ability to protect and defend themselves against the aggressions of the Navajos and Apaches, and, if permitted to form a combination of Pueblos, they could and would exterminate these tribes, especially every Navajo who should be so unfortunate as to be caught south of the high mountains north of the San Juan, a supposed tributary of the western Colorado, provided the government of the United States would furnish the necessary fire arms, ammunition and subsistence.[86]

But the request for firearms was denied by the authorities.

It is notable that the Zunis, while suffering from constant attacks by the Navajos, made the long journey to Santa Fe partly to ask "permission" to go to war—they were standing by their commitment to peace and their alliance with the U.S. government.

Cebolleta, a town seventy-five miles northeast of Zuni Pueblo, was occupied by the military in December 1849 as a protective garrison for the area. Negotiations began at once to obtain corn from Zuni to supply the fort. Despite this new military presence, again in January of 1850, Governor Pino informed the military of depredations against the Zuni people by Navajos—in this case the kidnaping of two women and the theft of mules and horses.[87]

On August 7 and 8 of 1850, the situation again forced Governor Pino and other Zuni officers to journey down the hard road to Santa Fe for a conference with Agent Calhoun. The agent had drawn up another treaty with the Pueblo Indians. He reported that the Zunis came "not only for the purpose of signifying their concurrence in the terms of the treaty proposed, and signing the same, but also for the purpose of urging the Commanding Officer of this Military Department to permit them to make war upon the Navajos."[88] It had been nearly a year since the treaty with Governor

Washington had been signed, and the Zunis had been waiting diligently for the government to honor its commitments. Pino's honesty and persistence in this particular effort is notable. Finally, the authorities relented, and "on this occasion," Calhoun wrote, "Col. Monroe has consented to their wishes, and has furnished them with powder and lead to a limited extent."[89]

Calhoun went on to record some of Governor Pino's complaints: "Within the last four weeks the Navajos have made two assaults upon Zuni. On the first assault, they killed two of the Zuni Indians, and on the second the Governor's Lieutenant was killed, and several animals were driven off."[90] The military command which had been stationed recently at Cebolleta had quickly been withdrawn because of Apache depredations, and the Zuni governor questioned the efficacy of United States military policy in the area since General Kearney's arrival.[91] Obviously referring to the treaties the Zunis had previously signed, which gave them the right to protection from their enemies by the government, Pedro Pino inquired, "How does it happen that at the very moment the Navajos are commencing a war against him (the Pueblo of Zuni), the American troops are *withdrawn* from Cebolleta?" He [Pino] answered, "I supposed to give the Navajos a *fair chance* against us— *who were promised PROTECTION*."[92]

The treaty which Pino came to Santa Fe to sign had been approved by the pueblos of Santa Clara, Tesuque, Nambe, Santo Domingo, Jemez, San Felipe, San Ildefonso, Chochiti, Santa Ana, and Zia during the month of July and was signed by Pino, representing Zuni, in August of 1850. The various pueblos promised not to give any aid or countenance to tribes which were at war with the United States and to treat all U.S. citizens humanely. Referring to Pueblo Indian lands, Calhoun intimated that precise boundaries of the pueblos were known by the government. Certainly Pino would have described the exact boundaries of Zuni land. The treaty resolved that "the Government of the United States will, at its earliest convenience, afford to the contracting Pueblos its protecting power and influence; will adjust and settle, in the most practicable manner, *the boundaries of each Pueblo, Which shall never be diminished, but may be enlarged whenever the Government of the United States shall deem it advisable*."[93] Pino would later complain that the

authorities in Santa Fe had promised him the exact boundaries of
Zuni land would be secure under U.S. rule. This must have been
one meeting where this promise was made.

The supply of powder and lead was put to efficient use by the
Zuni soldiers, evidenced when, on September 30, 1850, Calhoun
informed the commissioner of Indian affairs that a battle had
taken place in which the Zunis had killed thirty Navajos. But
Calhoun stated that the Navajos were not deterred and were plan-
ning another conflict.[94]

Finally, the authorities in Santa Fe complied with Governor
Pino's request for sufficient arms and ammunition to defend the
pueblo. On October 9, it was reported that the military commander had arranged for sixty flintlock muskets, an adequate
supply of flints, and six thousand buck-and-ball cartridges to be
sent to Zuni so that the people could defend themselves. Pino's
diplomacy had worked, but before the delivery was made, the
Navajos again attacked the pueblo.[95]

The Navajo party attacked the pueblo and began to burn the
cornfields. That would not have been possible if Zuni men had not
again been away from the pueblo, and evidently the contingent of
U.S. troops at Cebolleta was also busy elsewhere: The soldiers and
Zunis were escorting the bishop of Durango on a visit to Zuni. This
was Bishop Zubiria's third visit to the pueblo—he had been there in
1833 and 1845—and the Zunis had joined the escort to hack out a
road for the bishop across the Zuni Mountains.[96]

Calhoun, who had recognized that another attack on Zuni was
imminent, could also see the significance it could have on the
U.S./Zuni alliance and policy in the region. He reported to the
commissioner of Indian affairs on October 12 that if the Zunis
(now under attack) "have been able to save their crops, it will be
fortunate for our troops, as they relied upon them for a portion of
their supplies, which would have been greatly augmented if their
warriors could have been engaged in tilling the earth instead of
guarding the Pueblo." He went on to suggest that an agent be stationed at Zuni and ordnance facilities be built to increase the
amount of food which could be raised there.[97]

This trade relationship with the government was one which
Pino had worked hard to establish. The garrison at Cebolleta had

contracted for five thousand bushels of corn (at about two dollars a bushel) from Zuni in 1850. Corn was said to be abundant on Zuni land during this season, and Agent Calhoun's suggestion that an ordnance depot be built would have provided much more storage space. The agent whom he proposed should be stationed at Zuni would also have prevented unofficial acquisitions from the tribe, but neither the agent nor the depot was ever established.

The tribe, under the secular direction of Pino, had thousands of bushels of corn to sell at the time, even though they kept on hand at least a two-years' supply in case of drought or grasshopper infestation.[98] Without the support of the Zunis and their large fields of corn, the army's western New Mexico forts could not have survived this period. A few years later, as whites began to settle in the area, it became more advantageous for the army simply to take the land and grow its own corn, while allowing the enemies of the Zunis to molest the pueblo with little protection. But for the time being, the arrangement worked in favor of the tribe.

The attack on Zuni took place on about October 14. It turned into a siege and lasted for sixteen days before the muskets sent by Calhoun arrived on the scene. Pino signed for the arms and ammunition on October 30, agreeing to return the muskets on demand. Though the garrison of Cebolleta was only seventy-five miles away and the contingent of troops was with the bishop in the vicinity, the attack on the pueblo went on under the nose of the U.S. troops until the Zunis were supplied with their arms. When the muskets arrived, the Navajos retreated from the area around Zuni and again focused their raiding on the villages along the Rio Grande and Rio Puerco to the east.[99] Pino's diplomacy had brought about much-needed relief from attacks.

By early 1851, it became apparent to the U.S. command that a campaign against the Navajos was again necessary because their attacks against the eastern pueblos had become so persistent. Henry Dodge, later agent to the Navajos, traveled to Zuni to buy corn for the contingent of troops. He was able to purchase a thousand bags and reported that much more was available if needed. He further said that the Zunis could be used as auxiliaries with no remuneration necessary. But increased Apache depredations to the south of the territory caused Dodge to cancel the campaign.

While at the pueblo, Dodge reported that a recent Navajo attack had wounded one man and horses had been stolen from the Zuni tribal herd.[100] So the Navajo attacks had not altogether ceased, though they had lessened.

Despite Pino's efforts to make a true alliance with the U.S. command and end Navajo depredations, by 1851 Calhoun (newly appointed governor of the territory) reported that "during the past year the Navajos had been more successful in their depredations than at any former period—these outrages should be stopped."[101] The statement reinforced the suggestions made by Governor Pino (which, in turn, mirrored those his namesake had made in 1812). Fort Defiance would be set up in the vicinity of the Navajos' heartland, and Colonel Edwin Vose Sumner, now in command of United States forces in the territory, would attempt to keep the Navajos permanently in check—a policy the Mexican and Spanish governments had attempted with more success. It is easy to see just how important the Zunis' corn was during this period, not only because of the outlying garrisons but also because the only money in the territory was government money, and the only commodity was Zuni corn—the Zunis should have done very well. Calhoun, however, was for a more "humane" treatment of the Navajos, and rumors quickly spread that he was out to take the Pueblo Indians' lands from them. [102]

Sumner organized his command and set out in August, accompanied by Calhoun, on an expedition against the Navajos. With help from the Zunis and advice from Pino, the Americans set up Fort Defiance. Sumner told Pino he was "going to give the Navajos the devil,"[103] but the command had not gotten far from Zuni before they got into trouble. On leaving the pueblo, one of the troops reported that, "unknown to us, the Zunis had dug numerous holes, beside a deep ravine where the trail crossed, and placing in the center of them a sharp pointed stick, and over it laid a slight cover of dirt, to ensnare the Navajos."[104] Colonel Sumner rode into one and almost killed his horse. At the same time, the troop's herder ran his sheep into another hole, where three were killed and the troops had great difficulty in removing the remainder.[105]

The troops moved on, and Sumner ordered that Fort Defiance be established near Canyon Bonito with Major Electus

Backus as its first commander. Sumner went on with the remainder of his command and conducted an ineffective campaign in the Canyon de Chelly country.[106] While Sumner was setting up Fort Defiance and leading his troops through Navajo country, Governor Pino was entertaining a group of the troops which had been left behind at Zuni. The Zuni governor arranged for a dance, which he apparently wished the United States soldiers to see.[107]

There were other newcomers to the Zunis' land during this period. Exploring expeditions, such as the one led by Captain Lorenzo Sitgreaves, began to pass through the western New Mexican territory. On reaching the pueblo, they were met by Governor Pino, who tried to obtain a written record of each visit, arranged feasts and dances for them, and supplied them with guides through Zuni territory. The testimonials he gathered from these people uniformly praised the Zunis' outstanding hospitality and Pino's intelligence, integrity, and statesmanship.

Sitgreaves's group, along with some of the troops left at Zuni by Sumner, went west from the pueblo, attempting to find a suitable route to the Colorado River. A few days after leaving Zuni, near the Little Colorado and a few miles from the present site of St. Johns, Sitgreaves met a group of Coyotero Apaches, who were herding mules on their way to Zuni to trade.[108] Sumner eventually returned to Santa Fe to regroup, ordering Backus to keep pressing the Navajos from Fort Defiance.[109]

Backus and his new command at Fort Defiance were having considerable difficulties. Supplies were slow in arriving, and the men were engaged in heavy labor, preparing for the upcoming winter. But the Navajos did not seem to be openly hostile, nor did they resist the construction of the fort in their country. Early on, Backus arranged with Governor Pino to have the fort supplied with Zuni corn.[110] The Zunis complied and increased their crops accordingly. But the Navajos did not view the fort as a deterrent to their raids; they considered it rather a "protective buffer" which allowed them to raid Zuni without fear of reprisal.[111]

Backus arranged for a peace summit among the Navajos, Zunis, and Hopis. The leaders of the three tribes gathered at Canyon Bonito on October 26, 1851, and a treaty was agreed to by all of those present, who must have included Pino. Backus reported to Colonel Sumner the content of the agreement:

> The following verbal agreement was entered into, and being submitted to the main body of Indians, was accepted and confirmed by them.
>
> 1st The Navajo Indians, shall be at peace with and shall cease to molest or steal from, the people of the United States, the Mexican people, and our friends the Zuni and Moca [Hopi] Indians.
>
> 2nd The Navajo Indians, shall send three of the principal men of their nation, with an escort of United States troops, to the Department Head Quarters at the Moro [Fort Union], with full powers to enter into and conclude a lasting treaty of peace, between the people of the United States and the Navajo nation.[112]

This was the last recorded "treaty" with Pino and the Zunis. Although it was 1871 before the U.S. officially ended the policy of treaty making, there would be no further attempts to negotiate agreements with the pueblo of Zuni.[113]

During the five-year period from 1846 to 1851, Pedro Pino had signed four agreements with the United States government. None was ratified by Congress, and, in fact, only one—that of Calhoun in 1850—was probably even submitted. The others included the 1846 treaty with Doniphan, the 1848 agreement with Colonel Boyakin, and Backus's 1851 agreement. Although the treaties were quickly forgotten by government officials, Pino and the Zunis believed they had entered into lasting agreements. The 1846 treaty gave the tribe the right to govern itself. The 1848 agreement gave the Zunis the rights of personal property and freedom of religion, as well as promising protection. Calhoun's treaty suggested that the government was well aware of the tribal boundaries and that, although they might increase in the future, they would *never* be reduced. Finally, Backus's agreement ensured that the Navajos would not steal from the tribe, as the government had promised for years.

Pino, now in his sixties, with fifteen years of experience as governor, had every reason to believe that he had guaranteed the future rights of the Zunis: Their land was safe, they were to be protected, a valuable trade had been instituted. The people could practice their religious beliefs without fear of reprisal from the government. Pino had done a good job of negotiating these agreements, but the United States government paid the same attention to them as did the Navajos—they were ignored by everyone but the Zunis. Pino would learn in the coming years that every single point he had fought for in these councils was lost to the United States. We can only guess how much worse the situation could have become if Pino had not been in charge politically.

three
Further Warfare

Though the Navajos had been cautioned not to steal from the Zunis in the 1851 agreement, they were back at their old tricks within a few months. Governor Pino reported in May of 1852 that Navajos had stolen Zuni horses. The frazzled commander of Fort Defiance wrote to Pino, promising to try and retrieve the stolen animals.[114] In the meantime, Electus Backus was evidently having a difficult time determining the correct course of action in a troubled time. The political situation was complicated, and Backus made it worse. He cautioned the Zunis that if they recovered stock which had been taken by the Navajos before the October 1851 treaty, they would have to return it to the thieves.[115] In effect, the Navajos were continuing their raids against the Zunis, Fort Defiance was protecting the aggressors, and the Zunis could no longer legally pursue the Navajos or react defensively. To top it off, now Pino was being told the Zunis could no longer retrieve their own stolen stock.

Pino looked for help elsewhere. It was reported about the same time that the Zunis entered into an alliance with the Mescalero Apaches against the Navajos. The Mescaleros killed a prominent Navajo leader, and Backus reported that Zunis were penetrating Navajo country in their own raids.[116] The situation was deteriorating.

Backus was relieved of duty in August 1852 by Henry Lane Kendrick, who would prove to be a friend of the Zunis and whom Pedro Pino would fondly remember many years later.[117] Duty at Fort Defiance was considered the most miserable in the United States at the time, and Kendrick was faced with a war many decades old, but he did his best. Major Kendrick spent five years at Fort Defiance, becoming one of the few men to begin to understand the situation among the Navajos, but even he did not pursue a course completely satisfactory to Governor Pino. In early 1853, Kendrick worried that the army was becoming *too dependent* on the Zunis for the fort's corn supplies. Without those supplies, the post would have to be relocated. Kendrick opened a new route toward the settlements in April, giving as one reason the fact that it would "indicate to the Zunians that we are not at all dependent on them."[118] During the next month, he sent a wagon train to Laguna to purchase corn, saying that if the train did not return with a full load, it would "derange my plans in relation to the Zunias."[119]

Kendrick found that he *did* have to rely on Zuni for his supplies. He purchased corn from Zuni in November[120] and reported in December 1853 that he might not be able to purchase any corn from Laguna and would therefore have to depend solely on Zuni for those supplies.[121] The Zunis also worked closely with the troops in maintaining a shaky standoff between the warring parties, reinforcing patrols, and helping the army recapture stolen stock.

In November Navajos again raided Zuni, and the Zunis were reported pursuing them. Kendrick, in a letter to Governor Pino, asked the people to try and watch their stock more closely to prevent an incident which would precipitate bloodshed.[122] Obviously the army was nearly impotent when it came to maintaining peace. Pino informed Kendrick that Navajos were "dancing" (threatening war) at nearby Ojo del Oso (Bear Springs) because of a recent Ute attack.[123]

Both Kendrick and Pino faced additional problems in dealing with the Navajos. Since Fort Defiance was considered one of the worst military assignments in the United States at the time, Pino was asked to help with a related problem—desertions. Pino was offered a reward of thirty dollars each for any deserter he could catch. Kendrick was also frustrated by government policy. Depredations continued at Zuni and elsewhere, and Kendrick was as disappointed as Pino with the territorial government's policy of dealing softly with the Navajos.[124] The Navajos were boasting "that they only spared them [the Mexican farmers in the region] to save themselves the trouble of cultivating corn and raising sheep."[125]

Smallpox and other European diseases had a tragic effect on Zuni population. Zuni may have had a population of six thousand when Coronado arrived in the sixteenth century. By 1850 the population had been reduced to somewhere around two thousand. During the following fifty years, Zuni population would fall to slightly more than fourteen hundred. Inoculations finally began to be given to Zunis in the twentieth century, and population responded by rising.

During 1853 Pino reported that the pueblo was again suffering severely from a terrible epidemic of smallpox. The governor lost two nephews, and the tribe as a whole was decimated, losing hundreds of members. The tragedy did not stop Pino from calling a council and convincing the *caciques* that guides should be provided for A.W. Whipple's exploring expedition, however. Whipple had been sent out by the government to determine a practical railroad route from the Mississippi River to the Pacific Ocean.[126] The Americans were beginning to understand the importance of Zuni territory, which the Spanish and Mexican governments had seen before them.

It was not long after the Whipple party reached the pueblo, on November 23, 1853, that Pino appeared before the visitors. Baldwin Möllhausen, topographical draftsman and naturalist to the expedition, reported in his diary that the prospect "of establishing a direct connection with the coast of the Pacific seemed to strike them wonderfully, and it was not long after they were informed of it before Pedro Pino, the *Governador* of Zuni, made his appearance in state costume with two of his chiefs to introduce himself to us, and obtain further information concerning the direction of our journey. . . ." Pino went on to describe the epidemic and mention the deaths of his two nephews. He said that "he and his people were in great sorrow."[127]

The expedition leaders asked Pino for guides to the Little Colorado, for "the services of natives who possessed an intimate acquaintance with their own hunting-grounds would be of more avail to us now, than the knowledge of the most experienced trappers."[128] The Zunis responded by holding a council.

In a debate that Pedro Pino had held with the wise men of the town, it had been determined that the enterprises of the Americans, which tended to establish more direct and rapid communication between the pueblos and white settlements, were by all means to be promoted; and for this purpose, José Hatché was to guide our Expedition by the shortest and best route to the Little Colorado, whilst José Maria was commissioned to proceed, in company with another Indian, in a northwesterly direction to the Moqui Indians, in order to obtain from them guides for the next portion of the journey, namely from the Little Colorado to the San Francisco Mountains.[129]

José Maria was the "war chief" of Zuni, and the other Indian to travel with him was identified as Juan Septimo.

Since the signing of the Treaty of Guadalupe Hidalgo, there had naturally been much interest in Spanish land grants since the government had now formally acknowledged that it would honor them. In 1854 an act provided that, under the secretary of the interior, the surveyor general of New Mexico would investigate all land claims in the territory.[130] Thus, when Whipple and his companions in 1853 heard that Pino had some old papers in his possession, they asked to see them. "Climbing a ladder," Whipple said, "we entered a comfortable room where the old man and his family were seated by a fire." Pino's son, Patricio, brought the papers for Whipple's perusal. "Glancing at the manuscripts, they were found to contain a correspondence between the governor of New Mexico and certain priests that had officiated at Zuni. One was dated 1757. The old man declined giving them to us, saying that a long time ago they had been found in a corner of the old church, and had since been handed down from generation to generation, till now they were considered as insignia of the cacique's office."[131]

The Zunis guided the expedition through the Petrified Forest and across the Little Colorado, to the edge of their territory, but were unable to persuade Hopi guides to help the rest of the way because their villages were also enduring a severe plague of smallpox—even worse, apparently, than Zuni's epidemic. So the Zuni guides received their payment and returned to the pueblo.

Pino also discussed other matters with Whipple and his party while they were in Zuni country. Noting a sacred spring near the pueblo, Whipple asked Pino about its history. Pino replied,

We live in a country without acequias [irrigation ditches], and, for the growth of our crops, depend upon rain. To obtain this blessing from the Great Spirit it is necessary for us to perform the rites and observe the ceremonies of our ancestors. This spring has ever been held sacred to the rain god. No animal may drink of its waters. It must be annually cleansed with ancient vases, which, having been transmitted from generation to generation by the caciques are then placed upon the walls, never to be removed.

Pino went on to explain several Zuni traditions to the army officers and discuss some of the basic religious concepts of the Pueblo people. He expressed his desire for an alliance with the government and said that the Americans were "brothers" but the Mexicans were not, and they were therefore not allowed to watch the sacred dances of the Zunis.[132]

The friendly relationship with Fort Defiance continued throughout the following two years. Pino and Kendrick carried out much trade, and Kendrick, in return for Pino's support, did his best to protect the Zunis. As though Pino was not troubled enough at this point, with Navajo raids, an epidemic of smallpox, and the burden of organizing guides for the United States expedition through Zuni territory, it was reported in 1854 that flocks of New Mexican sheep were being grazed on Zuni land west of the pueblo. The Zunis were very upset, and so was Major Kendrick, who reported that the reason the flocks were there was because the owners believed that the government would reimburse them for losses sustained at the hands of the Navajos.[133]

Kendrick reported the grazing of New Mexican sheep in the area of Zuni in February, May, and December of 1854. New Mexico's Governor Meriwether had trouble defining the area occupied by the Navajos, saying it was difficult because they had never had any recognized treaty boundaries and they "claim all the lands not actually occupied by the whites." But he did say that no Navajos lived to the south of Zuni (evidence that the Zunis were protecting their boundaries) and that the Navajos' area was between the thirty-fifth and thirty-seventh parallels of north latitude.[134] The Navajo raids in the Zuni area tapered off during this period, with Kendrick at Fort Defiance and the Zunis better equipped militarily. But depredations by the Navajos did continue in other sections of the territory throughout 1854.

While Pino was supplying corn for Fort Defiance, the government was thinking of ways to restrict the depredations of the Navajos. In 1855 Governor Meriwether received authority to make a treaty with the Navajos to buy a sizeable portion of what he considered to be their territory. The treaty was signed at Laguna Negra on July 17, 1855, under conditions which approximated a riot. The treaty called for $102,000 to be paid to the Navajos in the years from 1855 to 1876. The treaty was never ratified,[135] but Pino must still have wondered why the government was paying its enemies, while trading with its allies.

But that was not the worst of the agreement. The area to be set aside for the Navajos was described as

> beginning on the south bank of the San Juan River at the mouth of the Rio de Chelly thence up the San Juan to the mouth of the Canado del Amarillo thence up the Amarillo to the top of the dividing ridge between the waters of the Colorado and the Rio Grande thence southwesterly along said ridge to the head of the main bank of the Zuni River thence down the north side thereof to its mouth or entrance into the Collirado [sic] Chiquito, thence north to the beginning.[136]

This description cut a chunk of thousands of acres of land out of the Zunis' territory. The land had been used by the Zunis for centuries; it had never been controlled by the Navajos. The government's own reports clearly showed that Navajos never went farther south than Zuni Pueblo. Those drawing up the description had little understanding of the area.

Pino must have been enraged. Not only had the Navajos been given land which belonged to the Zunis but they had been given permission to travel to the Zunis' Salt Lake to gather salt. The treaty, however, was unsatisfactory to just about everyone involved except the Navajos.[137] Henry Dodge, agent to the Navajos, reported that the proposed reservation was larger than they had expected and that following the signing, they had returned to "their homes very much delighted with the liberal treatment in the Territory and presents [given] them by the Governor."[138]

It is surely true that the Navajos were happy with the outcome of this treaty. After they had marauded Zuni for decades, failed to keep any treaty for longer than a few months, and watched the inaction of United States troops, they had apparently won a victory. Not only had they received promise of payment for lands lost (much of which they had never occupied in the first place) and a reservation larger than they had anticipated but they had also been ceded lands which belonged traditionally to their enemies, the Zunis and the Hopis.

Vague mention was made of the rights of the latter two tribes when the governor reported that the reservation excluded "the lands owned by the Pueblos of Zuni and Moqui and [the United States was] reserving to them all their rights and privileges."[139] Obviously neither Pino nor a representative of the Hopis had been consulted during the treaty negotiations. The government was also intending to give the lands of its allies to their mutual enemy.

Kendrick decided to visit the lands in question with Governor Pino.[140] Following his visit, between June and August of 1856, Kendrick realized that the Zunis might lose important land in the proposed exchange. Mentioning particularly the farming villages of Pescado and Nutria, Kendrick summed up the situation:

> I do not know by what other title than possession these lands are held, nor have I legal knowledge enough to know whether that be good against the Navajos, under the treaty of Laguna Negra. If there be any doubt about it, the present difficulty with the latter should, by no means, be permitted to pass without removing such doubt. It would be, in every way, most unfortunate to have the Navajos cultivate in these localities, and in such proximity to the Zunis; it would entail endless troubles upon our authorities and the greatest evils upon the parties concerned. Fortunately, these grounds are not at all necessary to any but the Zunis. If congressional legislation be necessary to confirm the Pueblo title to these lands, it cannot be too early nor too earnestly invoked.[141]

Kendrick also asked that a special agent be assigned to the Zuni district to help protect the Zunis and Hopis from Navajo aggression.

Kendrick had already been aware of the Zuni Salt Lake and now was becoming familiar with all of Zuni territory.[142] His defense of Zuni rights won him the respect of the people, and his name was remembered long afterward.[143] There were other reasons why Kendrick had to protect Zuni interests. Fort Defiance was being fed with Zuni corn. In 1856 the pueblo was supplying the fort with four thousand dollars worth of grain annually, at a rate of $1.35 per bushel. The Zunis not only had three thousand surplus bushels to sell to the army but the situation was stable enough that they were even trading with the Navajos.[144]

Pino's advice had been to ally with the United States. He had taken every opportunity to help government expeditions and patrols. He had arranged trade agreements with the fort, and, with Kendrick commanding Fort Defiance, his policy seemed to be paying off. Kendrick in turn was encouraging the Zunis to expand the area of their farmland and discouraging their efforts to maintain herds of draft animals. In a droll comment about the Navajos' thieving habits, he said it was not "desirable that they should have [draft animals]. The possession of many mules or horses will assuredly lead to a taste for roving habits, if, indeed, the Navajos do not rob them of all such animals."[145] Kendrick needn't have worried about the Zunis' "roving habits." They already had possessed the horse for centuries.

Despite the apparent peace and the relative advantages of trade, Pino and the Zunis were in the midst of hard times. The smallpox epidemic had reduced the pueblo's population to between thirteen and fourteen hundred.[146] Several hundred of the people must have died during the course of the recent sickness. And even though the Navajos were restricted from Zuni boundaries, they were by no means pacified.[147] Pino had met several effects of the influx of the Americans with moderate success, but another result of that pressure was about to be felt.

In October of 1856, Zuni was attacked by Apaches, probably Coyoteros. Recent years had seen trade and generally peaceful relations between the Zunis and the Apaches. But encroachments by Americans on Apache lands were pushing them, in turn, to pressure their Indian neighbors. It was nothing new to the Zuni to be attacked by the Apaches—in 1672 Apaches had destroyed Hawikku and its mission, causing its permanent abandonment.[148] Apache raiding had even caused the evacuation of the main pueblo of the Zunis around the turn of the eighteenth century. But in recent years, trade had dominated the reports of Zuni/Apache relations. The Apaches were not successful in their attack. The Zunis quickly raised a force of their own, pursued the Apaches, and recovered most of the sheep, killing one Coyotero in the process. Major Kendrick at Fort Defiance heard of the raid and left his post on November 16 with Navajo agent Dodge to make a patrol to the south of Zuni. Armijo, a Navajo leader, accompanied the party as it traveled to Zuni. There the group was joined by Zuni war chief Salvadore, who served as guide in the ensuing journey.

About thirty miles south of Zuni, near what was called Cedar Spring, Dodge and Armijo left camp early in the morning to hunt on the Zuni plateau. A large party of Mogollons and Coyoteros was returning toward the pueblo to avenge the death of the Coyotero killed by the Zunis. A small group of the Apaches apparently came across Dodge while he was hunting and killed him. Armijo and Salvadore helped search for Dodge, studied the tracks, and reported that the attackers were Apaches—probably Mogollons and Gilenos—but they could find no trace of Dodge before they were engulfed in a terrific snowstorm. The storm was so vicious that Salvadore, reportedly, could not find his way in this country that he knew so well.

The force of Apaches moved on and attacked the Zuni Pueblo on December 22, 1856, taking a heavy toll. The Apaches killed at least ten Zunis and stole about one hundred head of cattle and horses. There are indications that the hundred attacking Apaches surprised one of the outlying farming villages and not the pueblo itself, as reports spoke of Zuni bodies lying ten miles from the pueblo for some time before they were recovered at night.

On February 5, 1857, an army patrol set out from Fort Defiance to look for *Dodge's* remains. Lieutenant Howard Carlisle led the patrol, accompanied by the Navajo Armijo. When they reached Zuni, they were not given the same help they had received before. Salvadore and two or three other Zunis were asked to accompany the troop southward, but the Zunis refused. When the troops requested to purchase additional food supplies, they were also refused. Carlisle's report suggests that the Zunis were in the midst of a celebration or religious function. If the function was Deshkwi, [149] then there was ample reason for Governor Pino to refuse the soldiers' requests. The early Americans paid little attention to the religious beliefs of the Pueblo Indians, but this may not have been the only reason for refusing to help the army. Perhaps Pino was perturbed that so much attention was being given to the death of one Anglo while so little was warranted by the deaths of ten Zunis.

At any rate, Dodge's body was recovered on the Zuni Plateau. Historians conjecture that Dodge, who had good relations with the southwestern tribes (he had corresponded with Pino), might have been the one person who could have prevented the Navajo wars of the 1860s if he had lived. Dodge's one son may have been Henry Chee Dodge, who became the first chairman of the Navajo Tribal Council. But the facts surrounding the entire case are controversial and shrouded in some mystery. [150]

Army patrols went out in 1857 to avenge the death of Dodge, and again the troops requested support from the Zunis. The leader of the major expedition reported that the Zunis again refused to help, saying that they were too busy planting their crops and that at a later date they might make an independent excursion of their own. [151] Pino may have decided that the army was not handling things correctly and that tribal leadership of such expeditions would be more efficient. Kendrick may have been reacting to Pino's refusal when he suggested that it would be a good idea to take a group of leaders from the western tribes, including Zuni, to Washington. He hoped that the trip would prompt the Indians to exert a good influence on their neighbors. [152] Pino had a slightly different version of the story, saying he was offered the trip in return for his assistance to government expeditions. [153]

In 1857 Kendrick wrote to his superiors that it was not necessary to give presents to the Zunis, as was done with other tribes in the Southwest, because they made enough money selling supplies to the fort to buy their own farming implements. But he added that, considering the Zunis' hospitality and the efforts they exerted in the United States' favor, it might be polite to offer them tobacco. The Zunis expected that, he said. [154]

Kendrick was relieved of his command in May of 1857 after a tenure of five years, a long period considering the fort's distinctively bad reputation. Kendrick had exerted a strong influence on the Navajos to keep the peace. The situation in the area was already deteriorating as Kendrick left Fort Defiance. Shortly before his departure, he reported to the governor of New Mexico that the Navajos were rapidly growing more confident that they could overcome the Americans.[155] The new agent to the Pueblo Indians didn't help matters. He didn't understand the long-standing difficulties between the Zunis and the Navajos and attempted to resolve cases in an arbitrary manner. The lands of the Zunis came into further jeopardy.

Late in 1857, a disturbance occurred between the Zunis and the Navajos. The Zunis had discovered a number of Navajos stealing corn from their fields. According to reports, they killed one Navajo woman and appropriated the horses of the rest of the party. The new agent for the Navajos, William Harley, reported that "the difficulties between the pueblos of Zuni and the Navajo became so serious that action on my part became necessary." Harley was ready to leave for the pueblo with a detachment of troops, but before he could go, a delegation of Zunis, led by Governor Pino, arrived in Santa Fe. The delegation included the war chief and nine others who had come to try and straighten out the Navajo/Zuni difficulties. A council was held, and Harley determined that the "corn taken by the Navajos should be paid for, the woman killed to be paid for by the Zunias according to the Indian usage, and that the horses taken by the Zunias should be returned to their proper owners."[156]

Harley said that his decisions satisfied both the Zunis and the Navajos, but there is evidence that the outcome was not acceptable to the Zunis, who only returned a portion of the Navajo horses in the following month. Harley reported that "the pueblos of Zunia have surrendered to the Navajo a portion of the horses and will doubtless deliver the residue when they can find them, alleging as a reason why all were not delivered at the same time that a portion had escaped from them."[157] Shortly afterward Harley informed the governor of Zuni that he was also temporarily the pueblo's Indian agent. Surely Pino would have seen Harley's role as agent to two warring tribes as a conflict of interest.

four
Citizenship and the Zuni Land Grant

I n 1856 the general feeling by one faction of the New Mexico territorial people and courts was that the Pueblos were citizens and could vote—and also should be able to alienate their lands. This same group included many who were opposed to the large, important Spanish and Mexican land grants. Despite the fact that the United States Congress had guaranteed, through the Treaty of Guadalupe Hidalgo, that it would honor all legitimate grants, there was still a strong movement against them. This group held that the grants were unnecessary and even counterproductive to the aims of the United States government.

During this period, several plots to defraud pueblos of their grants were uncovered, including the famous Victor dé la Ó case at Acoma.[158] The territorial authorities had been empowered by Congress to study the Spanish and Mexican grants in the territory to determine which were legitimate. Sometime during 1856, or perhaps earlier, a representative of the territorial government, or someone purporting to represent it, approached some of the pueblos and asked for their land grants, saying they needed to hand them over so that Congress could approve them. The grants of some of the pueblos disappeared completely during this time. The grants of others seem to have been destroyed. Of the documents later submitted to Congress, a large portion were later determined to be spurious—forgeries. The document submitted later, which was supposedly the Zunis' Spanish land grant, was among these.

It may never be possible to determine what, in fact, happened to the Zunis' valid land grant(s), but when Pino learned

44

many years later that his people's land was not properly deeded, he remonstrated that after his delegation had been called to Santa Fe, he had left with the impression that the U.S. government had formally recognized Zuni boundaries, which included the land between the Zuni Mountains, the Allegros and Escondido Mountains, the Little Colorado, Twin Buttes (beyond the Petrified Forest and the boundary between Hopi and Zuni lands), Navajo Springs, and the Rio Puerco of the West. He claimed that the Mexican government had given a land grant to the pueblo which covered the traditional territory of the Zunis. This would have been consistent with Spanish and Mexican policy.

Pino consistently worked to help the Zunis maintain control of their territory throughout his career, and it is partly through his efforts that we can document the boundaries of Zuni land, how much of it was lost, and when it was lost. The land-grant problem was compounded by several factors. Many documents were lost by the U.S. territorial government in its early years. Many were taken by the retreating Mexican officials in 1846. The territorial government reported further losses throughout the nineteenth century. There were mysterious fires, including the one in 1892 which destroyed part of the New Mexico Archives. In 1869 and again in 1870, portions of the archives were sold as wastepaper.[159]

Plots to deprive Pueblo people of their grants surfaced at several of the towns. As already mentioned, Acoma's grant was discovered in the hands of an Anglo. There were other indications of plotting. The grants of Santo Domingo and Santa Ana were lost before 1856. The Indians of Isleta and Nambé testified that they turned their grant papers and documents over to United States officials of the Territory of New Mexico, but by 1856 these documents had either been lost or destroyed. Indians of the Tesuque, San Ildefonso, and Pojoaque pueblos testified that they had lost their grants to Mexican officials. Testimony taken from Isleta Indians in 1856 "shows that their grant had been deposited in the Archives of the Territory, and that a man named Miguel Antonio Lobato had told the Indians that not long before he had the grant in his hands; that it was in the possession of a man at Polaverda or Socorro."[160] This grant was also lost and never recovered.

The importance of the Pueblo grants was well known in the territory among non-Indians. Christopher (Kit) Carson, in his annual report as Indian agent to the secretary of the interior for 1857, stated,

> Allow me to urge the importance of a speedy action upon the several grants of land made to these Indians [pueblos] by the government of Spain. Those grants have received adjudication of the surveyor general of this Territory, and have been by him forwarded to Washington for confirmation by the government. Much annoyance is occasioned on account of the imperfect knowledge we have as to the limits and extent of these grants. And what is perhaps of more importance the confirmation of the grants would quiet the apprehensions of the Indians, who have on some occasions evinced a want of faith in the honest intentions of the government in regards to their lands.[161]

The agent to the Pueblo Indians, S.M. Yost, also commented on the status of their lands:

> There are difficulties almost daily presented for adjustment to the agent for the Pueblos, arising from the fact that the limits of the pueblo grants are not defined, and in many instances the titles not confirmed. The Mexican population, who manifest an unvarying disposition to impose upon the rights of the Indians and trespass upon their lands are constantly invading their premises. It is difficult for the agent to determine when their complaints are just, owing to the want of properly defined boundaries, and the absence of formality in the titles. Evidence of the genuineness of the titles of these Indians to their pueblos, in instances where the original papers of the grants from the Spanish government had been lost, was taken by my predecessor, and sent to Washington by the surveyor general of the Territory, with a view of having the titles confirmed by Congress. That body, however, failed to act upon them, the consequence of which is continued infringements of the rights of the Indians, and the annoyance to the agent. It is all important to the interests of the Pueblo Indians and the protection of their rights that these grants be speedily confirmed, and the boundaries of their lands distinctly marked.[162]

In the meantime, the governor was operating under the belief that the boundaries were secure. The surprising thing is that Pino and the Zunis were able to save any land. By the 1860s the Territory of New Mexico had come under the influence of what was later called the "Santa Fe Ring." If the Zunis' land grant had had trouble before the ring, it had even less chance to survive as this group of schemers spread in the territory. Put very simply, the ring was a group composed mostly of lawyers who profited at the expense of citizens in, among other things, land speculation. They rewrote land grants to increase their own fortunes and lands, which were monstrous in size and value. Naturally these men were very interested in any of the existing grants in the territory. Whether or not the Santa Fe Ring influenced the Zunis' land problems is difficult to say. It would take massive work to untangle the incredible web of deceit and corruption begun by the ring; its results still impact the daily life of the state.

It is clear that the disposition of the grants which had come to light and been confirmed by 1868 was to the Santa Fe Ring's benefit. These grants limited the Pueblo Indians' use of their land rather than guaranteeing their traditional holdings. The grants were sometimes written to guarantee land in addition to what was used traditionally, the minimum central core. The Spaniards and the Mexicans, who allied with the Pueblo Indians, allowed them to cultivate and plant as much land as they could. The Santa Fe Ring purchased some of the Spanish land grants (no involvement with Pueblo Indian grants has been proven), illegally enlarged them, and thus were able to withdraw many hundreds of thousands of acres of grazing land from use by both Mexican Americans and Indians in the territory.

Besides the description of Zuni land which Pedro Pino gave each time that he was questioned and which all indications show was correct, records report two other Spanish land grants. Frank Hamilton Cushing had interesting comments on a land grant for the Nutria Springs area. Cushing said that, following the Pueblo Revolt in 1680 and during the reconquest of 1692, when Don Diego de Vargas succeeded in reaching an agreement with the Zunis, a grant was issued for Nutria Springs.

The Zunis have a tradition, which has been recorded many times throughout the past century and tells the story of the Pueblo Revolt and the reconquest. According to the story, the Zunis did not kill the resident priest at Halona but allowed him to stay with the tribe on top of their sacred mesa, Dowa Yalanne. When Vargas arrived, the priest helped to arrange a peace. Cushing reported that a *cacique* named Francisco Pallé helped to save the priest and that "a Regal grant was made by Carlos II, of Spain, to the said Francisco Pallé, of all the lands for a league from the center of Nutria Springs, in return for his services during the rebellion."[163]

Cushing observed that during the final Navajo/Zuni battle over the Nutria Springs area, the deed to Francisco Pallé was destroyed by fire. Of course, the Zunis continued to farm in the Nutria area throughout the conflict, but after the Navajos were sent to Fort Sumner, the Zunis realized that in the future there might be some conflict over the title to the area: "Fearful that the absence of the grant mentioned, would cause disputes to arise relative to the validity of their title, the Zunis made application to the commanding officer of old Fort Wingate in 1868, and that gentleman, confident of their deserts wrote for them the following certificate and notice of preemption." At this point in Cushing's manuscript, it appears that he thought he could obtain the document, but apparently he could not because he finished as follows: "This remarkable paper, which the Zunis have fondly held to as their testimony of right is still preserved by the aged great great grandchild of Francisco Pallé, Jose Pallé."[164]

Matilda Coxe Stevenson, who was at the pueblo in the 1880s and again near the turn of the century, reported that the Pallé family was the "richest in Zuni" and that one member worked drying peaches from the Zunis' orchards.[165] William E. Curtis, in a book written in 1883, also referred to the Nutria grant. He said that it was possibly one of the parchment documents which the Whipple party saw in 1853 (one was dated 1757). He also mentioned that Cushing was "aware of the existence of some such documents in the tribe today, but as yet has not been able to secure them."[166] There is still discussion at the pueblo of Zuni concerning the Nutria Springs grant, but to date no copy has come to light.

However, recent research has provided additional evidence of such a grant from Spain. A letterpress book containing copies of the correspondence of William J. Oliver, superintendent at Zuni in 1909, contains a copy of a document dated 1868. Cushing reported that in 1868 the Pallé family went to the commander of Fort Wingate, fearful that their claim to the Nutria Springs area would not be recognized. He said that the commanding officer provided them with a certificate, documenting their claims. Although the original 1868 document has apparently not survived, the copy that Superintendent Oliver made in 1909 has. It reads as follows:

KNOW ALL MEN BY THESE PRESENTS.

That Jose Balla, John Balla, Antonio Balla, Juan Perea Balla, Jose Gonzales Balla Naturales of the Pueblo of Zuni, have with the consent of the officers of the pueblo of Zuni, they understand, taken possession of the ranch of the Nutries: this 10th day of January 1868, one thousand eight hundred and sixty eight and has admitted one Hundred more persons of the Pueblo of Zuni: under the same right and possession as the above mentioned persons: which names are appended in Roll hereto and which Ranch has belonged to the Balla family for over one hundred years—given by the King of Spain to Jose Francisco Balla: Great Grandfather of the first mentioned undersigned and which Ranch has the following lines from the Nutri Spring 2 Two Miles East, West, North, and South, which ranch lays within the Zuni Pasture Grant, but conceded to the Balla family apart from the Tribe of Zuni on account of services rendered to the Spanish Kings during the Indian revulsion against the Spaniards and being inheritance of the first mentioned Jose Balla undersigned voluntarily agrees and takes in the persons mentioned in Roll hereto in order to guarantee said persons a good right and possession as himself and his family for all time and duration.

In witness whereof the undersigned Officers and Balla family sign their name this 10th day of January One Thousand Eight Hundred and Sixty Eight—1868.

Approved:
Manuel X McCavan
Caciqui of Pueblo

Approved:
Jose Lionicio X Luiseis[?]
First Capitan di Guerr

Approved Jose X Mackett
Captain of War

Jose X Balla
John X Balla
Antonio X Balla
Juan Berea X Balla
Approved:
Juan X Septimo
Governor of Lajunia.

Heirs by inheritance and of Law in possession and under cultivation

In 1946 a Zuni man by the name of Halate Quanamito visited the United Pueblos Agency in Albuquerque twice, asking about a copy of a paper Agent Oliver had made in 1909 regarding the land around Nutria Springs. The agency reported it could find no copy of the document. Clearly this copy of the 1868 document was what Quanamito was searching for.[167] The Zuni land grant which has attracted the most attention is one of the so-called Cruzate grants. This spurious grant is dated 1689 and purports to give the Zunis four square leagues (a league is about three miles). The document tells of the attempts to reconquer New Mexico following the Pueblo Revolt of 1680. The narrative of the "grant" declares that in 1689 "Captain General Don Domingo Jironza y Petriz de Cruzate" captured and interviewed a Zia Indian by the name of Bartolomé de Ojeda. Cruzate was then in the process of reconquering the pueblos of New Mexico, and Ojeda had much information concerning the disposition of the people and lands of Zuni. Following the testimony of Ojeda, the document says Cruzate issued a grant to the Pueblo of Zuni. Ten other New Mexico pueblos were named in similar Cruzate land grants: Jémez, Acoma, San Juan, Picuris, San Felipe, Pecos, Cochiti, Santo Domingo, Zia, and Laguna.[168] We know today that the Cruzate grants are forgeries for several reasons. One, the countersignature on the grants is Don Pedro Ladron de Guitara, when it should be Pedro Ortiz Niño de Guevara. Two, both the signatures of Guitara and Cruzate have been judged counterfeit. Three, the grant to Laguna is dated ten years before the pueblo was founded. And lastly, some material in the wording of the Cruzate grants, especially the ones for Santo Domingo and Laguna, seems to have been lifted from the book *Ojeada Sobre Nuevo Mejico*, written by Antonio Barreyro (Barreiro) in 1832.[169]

Most of the Cruzate grants surfaced in the 1850s in New Mexico when the surveyor general began work to confirm or reject the land grants. Although Pino visited Santa Fe, discussed land with the officials many times, and steadfastly reported that the American officials were aware of the exact Zuni boundaries (as recognized by Spain and Mexico), there is no record of any Zuni grant being filed in the surveyor general's office until twenty years later. Pino assumed throughout the 1850s, '60s, and '70s that the government knew about the pueblo's boundaries. He had certainly told them enough times, and there are indications that documents were in existence to support his peoples' claims, but no documentary record exists. The Zunis' Cruzate grant, however, seemed to take on a life of its own.

In 1876 it was officially reported that the grant had been filed with the surveyor general's office.[170] Several copies of that grant document are still on file in Santa Fe. All are copies, and none are on parchment as an original would be.[171] On September 25, 1879, the surveyor general's office, under Henry M. Atkinson, approved the Cruzate grant as valid and gave instructions to make a survey of it.[172] In 1880 depositions regarding the grant were taken from then ex-governor Pedro Pino and ethnologist Frank Hamilton Cushing. They were asked about the location of the Zuni Pueblo in 1689. Both replied correctly that the Zunis at that time had taken refuge on Dowa Yalanne, the mesa southeast of Halona:wa. Because of that testimony, many people in later years falsely inferred that the Zunis had only occupied their present village for two hundred years, when in actuality they had lived there for many centuries previous to the twelve-year period (1680–1692) during which they temporarily maintained a defensive position on the mesa top.[173] Pedro Pino seems to have hedged on his age when he gave this deposition. He said he was fifteen years younger than other reports indicate.

The interest in the Cruzate grant ebbed until the mid-1890s. As the reservation included the area of the grant, the surveyor general's office didn't push for its patenting. In September 1896, however, the acting agent for the Zunis wrote to the commissioner of Indian affairs informing him that "all deeds, documents, etc., connected with the Zuni Pueblo grant were lost, and suggested that something might be done in Congress to secure confirmation of their title and give the Indians a patent." Two months later he wrote again to say that the papers had been found at the surveyor general's office.[174]

The secretary of the interior and the commissioner of Indian affairs investigated the Zuni land-grant situation in 1898 and decided that only a congressional act could solve it.[175] In 1899 the secretary of the interior responded officially to the problem: "The title of the Zuni Pueblo Indians," he reported, "to this tract of land [the four square leagues in the Cruzate grant], of which the tribe has been in possession for two hundred years, is still unconfirmed, and can be secured to them only by special act of Congress. A draft of the necessary legislation will be prepared for submission to Congress at its next session."[176]

In 1900 a bill was introduced to the House of Representatives to confirm title to the area in the grant. The commissioner of Indian affairs added a new note to the controversy when he said, "It is respectfully urged that the title in and to their land be confirmed to these Indians at the coming session of Congress, as all the title papers held by these Indians for land occupied by them for over two hundred years, were a few years ago accidentally destroyed by fire."[177]

The commissioner mentioned the fire again when he wrote a letter to the House Committee on Indian Affairs suggesting quick passage of the bill.[178] The bill did not pass, however, and in 1901 the secretary of the interior again requested congressional action and mentioned that "all the title papers were accidentally destroyed by a fire a few years ago."[179] The commissioner of Indian affairs reiterated the request, including the story of the fire, and in 1902 another bill to confirm title to the land was introduced and sent to the committee but never acted upon.[180] What fire this was, or even if there ever was a fire, we may never know.

The references could be to the 1892 fire at Santa Fe which burned part of the New Mexico Archives.[181] Or perhaps this is simply a case of error magnification through the bureaucratic process. Fortunately the land in question was already a part of the Zuni Reservation (formed in 1877) because the government was moving at a pace normally reserved for geologic change. There were, however, reasons which came to light later that explain the slow action on this grant.

Nothing more happened until 1927, when, in response to questions, the acting commissioner of Indian affairs gave a short history of the grant and mentioned that the Cruzate grants had been judged spurious some time before. Ironically, now that the grant was next to meaningless, Congress did act, apparently to be absolutely sure that the area inside the grant boundaries was clearly titled to the Zuni people. On March 3, 1931, Public Law No. 825 was passed, confirming the Zuni grant.[182] It had taken the government thirty years to find the spurious copies of the grant and another fifty-five years to confirm it. It is fortunate that the future of the Zunis was not determined by their Cruzate grant.

Interest in the grant continued at the pueblo, and in 1954 Governor Leopoldo Eriacho visited the BLM offices and reviewed the file of papers. A note on an envelope reads, "He said he had brought the papers contained in this envelope. He requested that the papers be given to no one since it had taken him two years to secure them, with the aid of the First Indian Commissioner.— March 9, 1954."[183] As the envelope is empty, it is unclear which papers Governor Eriacho was referring to, but probably they were copies of the spurious grant which had been found in the pueblo and deposited with the archives. Who forged the Cruzate grants? We will probably never know, but we can be sure of one thing: It was not anyone at Zuni.

A problem which corresponded with the land-grant situation was citizenship. The Pueblos had enjoyed a special status under Spain and Mexico. In some ways, the tribes were citizens, and in others they were wards. Most importantly, their lands were protected. When the United States gained control over the territory, there was a conflict over whether the Pueblo Indians could or could not alienate their lands. The courts pondered the problem throughout the nineteenth century, and in the Lucero decision of 1869 and the Joseph decision of 1876, the courts determined that Pueblo Indians were not wards of the government like other tribes and "were not considered Indian tribes within the meaning of existing statutes."[184] This made the Pueblos prime targets for speculators and capitalists. Every conceivable means was used to pry Pueblo land away from the Indians. It was not until the Sandoval decision in 1913 that the Supreme Court ruled that Pueblo Indians were indeed "Indians" and entitled to the same protection as other tribes.[185] Against such odds, it is remarkable that the Zunis survived as well as they did (although today they possess less than a tenth of the land they once owned). Most of the Pueblo Indians ended up with only a tiny fraction of their Spanish and Mexican holdings.

A comparison can be drawn between the Pueblo Indians from 1846 to 1913 and the small western farmers and ranchers of today. Small farmers cannot prevent the giant utilities from putting their monstrous power poles through the middle of the farm, nor can the Montana rancher prevent companies from stripping the coal from his land—the huge corporations either have eminent domain or something nearly the same, not to mention the financial resources. The coal companies and power companies can get the land they want. Whether through bribery, manipulation, legal channels, or outright payments, the giant companies have the ability to get what they want today in the West (or almost anywhere else).

The Pueblo Indians were in a similar, if not worse, situation. Their allies were few. Their resources were few. To make matters worse, they had additional problems due to inaccurate translation and the fact that their records were often oral, not written. Thus, Pedro Pino had a positive effect on the relations at Zuni. He not only spoke Spanish articulately but Navajo as well. He also understood the importance of papers and kept every record he could— *even though he could not read them!*

During the sixty-seven-year period during which the Pueblo Indians were so vulnerable (1846–1913), calculated attempts were made to manipulate the public through misleading political dialogue. Then, as today, men who called for "equal rights" with the Pueblos were usually only after Indian land and really meant that rights currently held by the Indians should be taken away from them. During Pino's tenure as governor of Zuni, the trend was set for the pueblo. Despite the fact that the majority of Zuni land was lost to whites, the pueblo successfully retained the heartland of the area. The major springs of Nutria, Ojo Caliente, and Pescado were all saved. Undoubtedly, the fact that Zuni was one of the western pueblos was in its favor in the United States period.

But Pino's untiring efforts during this period were also of the utmost importance to the destiny of the pueblo. He *did* understand statesmanship. He *was* honest in his dealings with the United States (there has never been a battle between the Zunis and the U.S., and, in fact, the last recorded battle between the Zunis and any Europeans was against Coronado in 1540). Pino beat his head against the bureaucratic wall. Tirelessly he fought for his people's land. From Pino's perspective, it must have looked as if the government gave land to the warring tribes and ignored its allies, those tribes like Zuni which had been its friends throughout; that the government consistently took the easiest way out of a difficult spot; that the enemies of the government, like the Navajos, continually came out of the political fight on top.

It becomes all the more important to recognize the moral authority with which Governor Pino spoke and acted. He acted in good faith. He did not know all the twists and nuances of the pueblo's grant and his people's citizenship. Nor did the general public (even today the public has little understanding of Indian affairs). It is this author's belief that Pino's efforts helped the tribe to gain what it did. There is no way of knowing what would have happened if he had not been there, or if someone else had been in his place. But his efforts helped to salvage what land the tribe retained and, almost as importantly, to document what was taken and how. Pino did not knowingly compromise his own or his people's moral position or traditional method of dealing with foreign governments. At the same time, he was a sophisticated and honest statesman.

five
"Entangling Alliances"

Governor Pino would have been in his mid-sixties in 1857. He must have been secure in his belief that the United States would honor his people's holdings. He had invested more than ten years of negotiations in guaranteeing Zuni land claims. Every indication would have suggested that his people's land would be safe and his diplomacy would end in success. His people's friendliness toward the whites would be repaid. But things began to deteriorate toward the end of the 1850s. Whites were moving into the area in greater numbers, although they still did not encroach on Zuni land. And the Navajos were becoming bolder and bolder. Pino continued on, patiently dealing with all the new interlopers.

While numerous newcomers came through Zuni territory in 1857, the most memorable event must have been Edward F. Beale's road-building effort. Along with the command were seventy-six camels, being tested by the army for use in the deserts of the American Southwest.[186] We have no record of the Zunis' reactions to the cavalcade, but some Indian villages in the region mistook Beale's company for a circus.[187]

At Zuni Beale met with Governor Pino and, like those before him, began to negotiate for supplies. Beale was able to obtain seven hundred and fifty pounds of corn for each one of his camels, or twenty-eight and a half tons.[188] It is again evident that the early American explorations of the region would have been much more difficult without the help of the Zunis.

Though the Zunis had sufficient corn to trade to Beale, they were by no means having an easy time during this period. Beale passed on to the Colorado River and returned via Zuni in the summer of 1858. On that occasion, he reported that "here I bought corn, of which these Indians have plenty, for our mules. They [the Zunis] were all in great trouble, the Navajos having stolen one hundred and fifty of their horses." Despite the fact the Navajos were raiding the Pueblo, Beale was able to report that fine crops were being grown by the Zuni people, including extensive wheat fields at Pescado, which Beale passed on his way to El Morro.[189]

American emigrants to California began to try the route which led through Zuni. In July of 1858, one of these groups hoped to follow Beale's route across what is now Arizona. One of the members of the group commented on the situation at Zuni Pueblo when they passed through, reporting that the Zunis "raise much wheat, corn, beans, pumpkins, melons and stock—so much that they have a surplus to sell to the American Army."[190] The author, John Udell, also said that the Zunis were assisting the government in the war against the Navajos. Obviously Governor Pino was continuing to educate various Americans by explaining the history and present situation at the pueblo. Udell also reported that the Zunis claimed to have a grant for their pueblo which dated from the seventeenth century.

The Udell train didn't make it across the western desert beyond Zuni. They were attacked by Mohaves and had to limp back to the pueblo, arriving on October 20, "in a starving condition."[191] The Zunis nursed them back to health, providing bread, beans, "fine" pumpkins, and a large room where they could recuperate from their ordeal. Udell remarked on the hospitality of the Zunis and also reported the first evidence of a permanent trader at the pueblo.

Ezra Bucknam was the trader, who was described by Udell as an "American, from the Eastern States, and . . . quite an intelligent man—a trader with these Indians. He acts in the capacity of interpreter for us."[192] Bucknam wrote to the officials at Fort Defiance describing the emigrants' condition and the efforts of the Zunis to help them recover. Then, apparently at the prompting of Governor Pino, Bucknam reported a problem that the Zunis were facing. He said that "several days ago a Navajo came in here and said his people would in a few days bring in a captive they had taken from here about a month ago on the 6th. Three Navajos came to the Mountains bordering this valley on the north and made a signal. The captive at the same time they turned loose who came safely home." Evidently the show of good faith by this group of Navajos did little to influence the hearts of the Zunis, for "nine Pueblos immediately set out and they say they shot one of the Navajos through the belly, but did not get him."[193]

It is interesting that the Zunis had a completely different attitude toward another Navajo who wished to come and live at the pueblo and evidently wanted to be adopted into the tribe. Bucknam also questioned the authorities, on behalf of Governor Pino, about the possibility of allowing this Navajo to join the tribe. "There is a ranch," Bucknam wrote, "somewhere to the northwest of here some 25 or 30 miles where several families of Navajos live." Though the mileage is incorrect, Bucknam is likely referring to Ojo del Oso, or Bear Springs, in the Zuni Mountains, where the Zunis had allowed a small group of Navajos to settle. "One of these Navajos," Bucknam continued, " has been here several times since the commencement of the war to obtain permission of the pueblo to bring his stock and live here. The Pueblos have asked my advice about it and I advised them not to permit it, as the war is declared against the nation and they cannot contract peace with any part of it without making themselves responsible (will you please give me your views upon this point?)."[194]

Bucknam translated the reply of the commander in charge of the Navajo campaigns, Lieutenant Colonel Dixon Stansbury Miles, for the governor of the Zunis. Pino heard a blunt report from Miles.

> You state you have a Navajo settlement near you; get the Zunians to break it up and kill all the warriors. I would like the women saved for I believe now through them only can I obtain peace, and I would like you to instruct the Zunians, I want all the women brought in here as prisoners, not to kill them. That the Zunians and Coyoteros are invited to war on these Navajos, *until I say stop*—strip them of everything and kill all they catch. Keep them running.[195]

So Pino was told it was not all right for the tribe to accept refugees. The government still had not learned that the Navajos were not united under any one leader, that there were many groups scattered over an area of northern New Mexico and Arizona under several different heads. The Navajos in question probably had never been at war; otherwise the Zunis would not have allowed them to settle on their land. The Zunis were told to kill *all* Navajos. But the Zunis' beliefs would not allow them to follow these orders from the United States, and Governor Pino, as we shall see shortly, was put in a position of defying the government's orders.

For trader Bucknam, it was "love at first sight" with a woman among the emigrants who were recuperating at the pueblo. Udell reported that on November 1, 1858, he married Mr. Ezra Bucknam to Miss Adaline Daily. Mrs. Bucknam would later cause considerable trouble for Pedro Pino and others at the pueblo, but in the meantime all was bliss. Following the wedding, the emigrant group minus Mrs. Bucknam, after fourteen days in the Zunis' care, returned toward Albuquerque.[196]

Throughout that year, 1858, the Zunis were allied with the United States in a campaign led by General Miles. Although the Navajos could attack the Pueblo Indians for years on end, and the government would not respond, when the Navajos stole the horse of an officer of the army, a war was likely to start. Apparently the government responded to deprivations by the Navajos against only a select few. Although the grievance in 1858 was certainly a great deal more serious than a stolen horse, reports of the war indicated the government's attitude toward New Mexico's Indian population.

The 1858 campaign was precipitated when a Navajo rode into Fort Defiance and shot, in cold blood and for no apparent reason, a young black slave belonging to one of the officers. The army responded. William P. Floyd, a surgeon under Beale who was stationed at Fort Defiance, recorded some terse words about the army in his diary. "Congress," wrote Floyd,

> had better disband the Army, dismiss all Indian agents and let out keeping the Indians quiet by contract. As the Post Office is managed, it would have money and be more efficiently done. The life of no citizen is protected by the Army and the death of none has been avenged by it. The Navajo war, it is true, was caused by an Indian killing a *negro*, but he belonged to an offi-

cer of the Army and was private property, not a citizen; so much for the army.[197]

The 1858 campaign began in September, and the principal guide and leader of the Zuni contingent was identified as José. This was likely José Maria, who was called the first war chief of Zuni for many years but whose real title was probably head priest of the bow. José Maria led the troops for some time as Miles's progress ebbed and flowed. On September 24, 1858, an account by Indian Agent S.M. Yost was published in the *Santa Fe Weekly Gazette.* Yost's smug account went as follows:

> The principal guide of the troops is a Pueblo Indian from Zuni. It was with some difficulty at first that any one of the Pueblos could be obtained. Finally this one consented. He is a small, erect, well-formed Indian and wears his thick raven hair hanging down to the middle of his back. He now is dressed up in citizen costume, including hat and shoes, and is withal a rather noted personage. In the scout to the Canon de Chelle [*sic*] one of the prisoners taken was handed over to the Mexicans and the guide to be disposed of. It was agreed that Zuni should be the executioner. The Navajo was soon placed at a short distance off, when Zuni raised his old flint lock fusee to do his duty. Navajo appealed—O don't kill me, my friend! Zuni very gravely responded—Por que, porque?—why not, why not? This very rational and reasonable question not being satisfactorily answered to Zuni's notions of the ethics of war, he took deliberate aim, and sent a leaden messenger through Mr. Navajo's brain, thus ushering his untutored spirit into the blissful regions of the great hunting ground. Zuni was very much delighted with the amusement, and says he will be made a big chief when he returns home.[198]

Yost's account deserves some attention. Beginning with his description of José Maria, Yost reveals some of the basic misconceptions and prejudices of the Americans. Yost correctly states that the Zunis did not want to be involved in the alliance and that there was "some difficulty" in getting Maria to join the campaign. Then Yost describes Maria. He reports that Maria was "dressed up in citizen costume." Had Yost been more informed, he would have said that the citizens of the territory were largely "dressed up in

Zuni costume"—cotton had been grown in the pueblos for centuries. When the command ordered Maria to execute a Navajo, Yost deemed it important to comment on Maria's "ethics of war." Finally, Yost displayed all of his prejudice in his description of the Navajo's death. "Amusement" is Yost's word, and it aptly describes the flight of fantasy in his rendering of the scene.

In October of 1858, a party of one hundred and sixty Zunis, led by Governor Mariano and four war captains, joined the Miles command, giving as their reason for going to war "to get back their loot and stolen horses."[199] There are several explanations for the apparent break in Pino's long term as governor of Zuni. It may have been that Pino was removed from office by the *caciques* because they did not approve of his policies—the record indicates that Pino consistently took the peaceful option when confronted with diplomatic alternatives. It may have been the consensus among the *caciques* that war was necessary, and so a more militant leader was made governor. Another possibility is that Pino was ill and unable to do a proper job with the heavy responsibilities of the governor. Or it may have been simply that the U.S. authorities gave an incorrect title to Mariano. It was not uncommon for Pueblo Indian leaders to be called "governors" no matter what their real title was. In fact, the recording of Indian names by whites was so haphazard in those days in the territory that Mariano may also have been José Maria. The latter is the more likely possibility. At any rate, the break in tenure for Pino was brief, and he was back as governor within the year.

There was considerable action during the 1858 campaign, for which the Zunis received both praise and condemnation. About midmonth in October, a party of three hundred Navajos attacked twenty-five soldiers near the mouth of Conyoncito Bonito. The Zunis, who were camped nearby, came to the troop's assistance and drove the Navajos off, for which they were commended by the authorities. During the engagement, the Navajos had three men killed but escaped with sixty-two army mules. The army had two killed and four wounded, but if the Zunis lost anyone, it was not reported.[200]

During the entire campaign of 1858, the Zunis captured a hundred horses and five head of cattle and killed one Navajo, while reporting only two wounded among their ranks. The one hundred and sixty Zunis burned the village of Navajo leader Manuelito, where they captured the Navajo ponies. But Miles criticized the Zuni soldiers for not following his orders. The record shows that the Zunis inflicted all the damage on the Navajos during this conflict, and Miles may have been revealing his frustration when he criticized their troops.[201]

Between twenty and sixty Navajos were killed during the 1858 hostilities. Late in the year, an ill-advised armistice was hastily arranged between the Navajos and the United States, and then another treaty was signed. The negotiations and the treaty were ill conceived and badly executed. Again the Zunis were not even consulted—although they had sent their own men to fight beside the white soldiers. And again the United States, through this treaty, intended to give land which belonged to the Zunis, their allies, to their enemies, the Navajos.[202] Though the document was as worthless as the other treaties with the Navajos, the agreement naturally incensed Governor Pino.

In 1859 Beale was again out on a reconnaissance, this time to find a wagon road from Fort Smith to the Colorado. Udell's company of emigrants joined Beale, making another try to reach California. Several weeks before reaching the Pueblo, Beale sent two wagons ahead to Zuni to obtain corn. Beale anticipated trouble in obtaining the supplies but in fact acquired a sufficient quantity [203]—two wagon loads of the Zunis' "splendid crops of corn."[204]

Knowing he would be back through the pueblo, Beale had left some goods with Governor Pino the year before. The Zuni governor greeted Beale as he arrived. Beale reported,

> The old governor met me in the town with many compliments and congratulations, and bearing in his arms a box containing my "artificial horizon" [surveying equipment? or maps?] which I had left with him in passing last winter. He told me the charge had been a great burden on his mind, and he was glad to be rid of the responsibility; rewarding him with several blankets and numerous pieces of calico, I sat down in his house to hear the news.[205]

Beale's advice to Governor Pino differed greatly from what Miles had told him the previous year. Beale reported that Pino "had a long list of grievances. The United States had persuaded him into an alliance with the troops as auxiliaries in the late war with the Navajos; his people had fought with our troops side by side like brothers; the United States had found it convenient to make peace with their enemies, and had left their auxiliaries the prey of their powerful and numerous foes." Beale responded: "I told him I thought it served him right for meddling in things which did not concern him, and warned him for the future to avoid all entangling alliances."[206]

Although it was up to Pino to decide the proper political course of action for the pueblo, the government was not making it easy. First, the army went to considerable effort to involve the Zunis in the military campaign, and then a commander of the same army told Pino it had been a mistake for him to allow his people to be implicated. The government would continue to work at cross-purposes at Zuni (and with other tribes) for the next hundred years: giving contradictory advice and orders; encouraging, consciously and unconsciously, divisiveness among members of the community; and making it almost impossible for the tribe to make the correct political decisions.

But Beale praised Governor Pino before he left Zuni. His tribute to Lai-iu-ah-tsai-lu also contradicted his previous criticism about Zuni trade: "I have given this letter to the governor of this indian Pueblo, it being my third visit and being dealt fairly with by him and his tribe, always willing and ready to trade on reasonable terms, I recommend all Americans to do him justice, and be honorable in their trading with him."[207]

Almost with the clockwork of the natural seasons, the Navajos attacked Zuni again in the spring. The attack came in March 1859,[208] and perhaps it was this attack that prompted the killing of a Navajo who visited the pueblo the same spring.[209] In August the Zunis reported another raid in which thirteen head of oxen and cows were stolen by Navajos and driven into the Chusca Valley. United States troops were unable to retrieve the cattle. In fact, the army found itself unable to provide the protection for Zuni for which it was obligated. And Zuni itself, by diverting its attentions to provide farm commodities for the troops, was less prepared than it should have been.

The Navajo Indian agent, Alexander Baker, aware that the army was not doing its job, informed Governor Pino that he should kill any Navajos in the area. In a letter to his superior, Baker described his discussions with Pino: "I have given to the Governor of the Zunia Indians written permission to kill all the Navajos that go among them without a written passport from me; first to order them to leave their place; then, if they would not go, to put my request in execution, that will be the best way to protect themselves and their property. The Governor tells me they [the Navajos] never come there that they don't steal something when they leave."[210] Baker also reported that Navajo leader Zarcillos Largos was present when Pino was given this license.

The Zunis were evidently still successfully protecting their borders in 1859. During that year, a concerted effort was made to determine the main positions of Navajo occupation. One party, led by Captain O. L. Shepherd, explored the southern area of Zuni territory. After traveling through the area of the Zuni Salt Lake and Rito Quemado, Shepherd concluded his report by stating, "Judging from the absence of signs on the route from the Acoma Mountains to the Pueblo of Zuni, the Navajos do not frequent the region south of the Zuni Mountains, although the climate is warm and the pasturage abundant during the winter months."[211]

While the Zunis took care of themselves, the army was losing patience with the Navajos. By the end of 1859, the Navajo agent, having tried everything he could think of to force that tribe to comply with its treaty obligations, applied to the military commander to use force against them.[212]

At the pueblo, other problems were receiving the attention of the governor and secular authorities as the year ground to a close. Trader Bucknam and his wife raised a stir over an incident at the store. It was reported that Zunis and Apaches visiting the pueblo to trade for goods would while away the hours drinking and smoking in the trader's backroom. On January 26, 1859, Ezra Bucknam accused Zunis of "an attempt to outrage the person of Mrs. Bucknam."[213]

The commander of Fort Defiance acted quickly, hurrying to Zuni and arresting two men. The Zuni prisoners were manacled and taken over the long road to Fort Defiance. Then an investigation took place. The Navajo agent reported that Adeline Bucknam had apparently stepped outside for a breath of fresh air as the various men smoked and drank in Bucknam's back room. One of the Zunis stepped out as well and approached her. He placed a hand on her shoulder and said, *"Muy bonita mujer"* (literally "very pretty woman").

"This," the Navajo agent concluded, "seems to be the offense."[214] Surely Governor Pino must have wondered at the American way of justice. When the New Mexico superintendent of Indian affairs determined that Bucknam was at Zuni illegally, carrying out an illicit business, he decided the penalty should be removal. This much was good, but Bucknam continued to trade with Pueblo Indians. He was allowed to move and open a new store at the Pueblo of Laguna![215]

"Indian Altar and Ruins of Old Zuni." This lithograph from a drawing by Baldwin Möllhausen depicts a shrine on top of Dowa Yalanne, near the ruins of the village there used by the Zunis from 1680 to 1692 as a defensive refuge after the Pueblo Revolt. The image accompanied a report by Thomas Ewbank in the *Reports of Explorations and Surveys to Ascertain the Most Practicable and Economical Route for a Railroad, 1853–54,* published by the 33rd Congress, 2d Session (S. Doc. 78) in 1856.

Looking southeast from Zuni Pueblo towards the Zunis' sacred mesa, Dowa Yalanne, ca. 1879. Photograph by John K. Hillers. National Archives, 106-IN-2384CF.

Half of an 1873 stereoscopic image of the Pueblo of Zuni by Timothy
O'Sullivan, when with George M. Wheeler's Corps of Engineering
expedition.

Pueblo of Zuni in 1873. Note the walk-in wells in the foreground.
Photograph by Timothy O'Sullivan. National Archives, 77-BC-129.

An early photograph of the old Catholic church at Zuni. Photograph
by George Ben Wittick, ca. 1880. National Anthropological Archives,
Smithsonian Institution, 02425200.

Seated on the left, Patricio Pino (Ba:lawahdiwa); on the right, Pedro
Pino (Lai-iu-ah-tsai-lu). Photograph taken at Zuni in 1879 by John K.
Hillers. National Anthropological Archives, Smithsonian Institution,
2255A.

Patricio Pino (Ba:lawahdiwa), son of Pedro Pino, and governor of
Zuni when this photograph was taken (probably 1882) by John K.
Hillers. National Anthropological Archives. Smithsonian Institution,
2230A

"Zuni Sacred Spring." The spring was inundated by a dam built by the United States government in the early twentieth century. This lithograph accompanied a report by Thomas Ewbank in the *Reports of Explorations and Surveys to Ascertain the Most Practicable and Economical Route for a Railroad, 1853–54*, published by the 33rd Congress, 2d Session (S. Doc. 78) in 1856.

"A Zuni Cornfield with its Scarecrows," drawing by Frank Hamilton Cushing, 1884. From Cushing, *Zuni Breadstuff* (New York: Museum of the American Indian, 1920).

"Plan of a Zuni Cornfield" by Frank Hamilton Cushing, 1884. Note intricate use of check dams to move water throughout the field. The inset in the upper right illustrates Zuni prayer sticks and the inset at the bottom shows a Zuni praying to consecrate the field. From Cushing, *Zuni Breadstuff* (New York: Museum of the American Indian, 1920).

A Zuni "waffle garden." From a stereoscopic photograph taken by
Timothy O'Sullivan in 1873. Vegetables such as peppers, onions, and
garlic were grown in these carefully tended gardens, watered by
hand. Photograph National Archives, 77-WF-41.

"War Chief of Zuni Indians" (possibly José Maria) in 1873. From a
stereoscopic photograph by Timothy O'Sullivan. National Archives,
77-WF-44.

A Zuni war-victory dance, as photographed by Timothy O'Sullivan in 1873. National Anthropological Archives, Smithsonian Institution, 02410300.

six
The Navajo War

T he inevitable all-out war with the Navajos finally came during the 1860s. After the commander of the army in New Mexico, Colonel Thomas T. Fauntleroy, reduced the forces at Fort Defiance by nearly two-thirds in November of 1859, the Navajos perceived the weakened condition of the post In January of 1860, nearly a thousand Navajos boldly attacked Fort Defiance. The engagement left three U.S. soldiers and nine Navajos dead and prompted the secretary of war in Washington to order a major operation against the Navajos. During the same spring, Navajo war parties stole sheep, horses, and asses from Zuni Pueblo.

Navajo raids against the settlements, and especially Zuni, increased throughout the year. The Navajos killed many and stole a great deal of property in 1860. During the winter, they raided Zuni again, prompting the tribe to send out two war expeditions and plan more. A fort was finally established in the vicinity of Zuni Pueblo, but with the Civil War approaching, it is not surprising that the Zunis were subject to more, not fewer, depredations from their old adversaries.[216] Indeed, there are indications that building the fort at Ojo del Oso was in some ways a hindrance to the Zunis because the Navajos again viewed it as a protective buffer to hide behind and not a discouragement against raiding.

Governor Pino fought with the United States during this period, but the efforts of the army to protect the pueblo were far from adequate. In November 1860, the command of the western forces in New Mexico was moved to the post at Ojo del Oso because of reports about Navajo movements to the west of Zuni and near the Little Colorado. A depot was set up near the pueblo for winter use, and Navajos were detected at Jacob's Well and Navajo Springs, but Navajo prisoners denied any knowledge of the Little Colorado. Despite the close presence of United States troops, the Zunis began to suffer more and more Navajo attacks. The agent to the pueblos, Silas F. Kendrick (not to be confused with Henry Lane Kendrick), stated in his annual report for 1860 that "for several months past, the Pueblos have suffered great and frequent losses by the depredations of the Navajos. The villages of Laguna and Zuna [sic] have been the chief sufferers. . . ."[217]

Pino and the other secular leaders of the various pueblos were faced with complex problems and strained to reach sophisticated decisions. The government had talked about giving presents to the Pueblo people, but a number of policies bothered the Indians. Some pueblos refused to take any farming implements as gifts because they could not be distributed equally. If everyone could not receive a tool, no one should have one—evidence of a strict cultural belief in economic equality. Silas F. Kendrick reported another worry of the Pueblos:

> . . . designing Mexicans had impressed them with suspicion that, although the government proffered to give them these presents, yet that some day they would be called on to pay for them, and that the debt thus raised against them would be converted into a claim against their lands. This apprehension was more strongly impressed upon their minds, from the fact that their grants and title papers which have heretofore been placed on file in the office of the surveyor general for confirmation, have never been returned to them, nor any patent from the government issued for their possession.[218]

In point of fact, when in the 1950s cases finally began to go before the Indian Claims Commission, the government did use any recorded gifts made to Indians as a deduction against judgments they might receive for lands taken unconscionably.

Kendrick went on to observe the quality of the Pueblo government:

> The Pueblos have governmental institutions far more ancient, and as firmly established as any other people, whatever, upon this continent. Each village, or "Pueblo," as it is called, is a political

community of itself, has its own complete organization; its own laws; its own tribunals, has its officers for their enforcement. Probably there is no people, enlightened or otherwise, among whom the laws are enforced with greater regularity and efficiency. That these laws are adapted to their condition and in the main promotive of their happiness and prosperity, their material condition and the absence of discontent conclusively testify. It would be no boon to them to convert them into citizens, and leave them within the operations of the civil code of this Territory. On the contrary, such a policy would probably result in their destruction.[219]

Pino and the Zunis carried on in spite of the increasing attacks and managed, further, to protect their borders. A drought, disease, and constant Navajo attacks left the Zunis weak in numbers but not in spirit. During the latter part of 1860 and the early part of 1861, operations were carried out against the Navajos in their hiding places in the Zuni Mountains, on mesas bordering the Rio Puerco, in the Chusca Valley, and in the area between the Rio Puerco and the Hopi villages. Reconnaissance of the region around the Puerco of the West suggested that most Navajos were on the far side of the river from Zuni.

The Zunis responded to every attack by the Navajos. In late January, Navajos stole mules from Zuni and escaped into the mountains. Army patrols pursued the raiders, but when they arrived at the Navajo camp, they found that Zunis had already attacked, leaving three Navajos dead after apparently recovering a portion of the stolen stock. Despite the assiduous protection of their borders, by February 1861, the Zunis were beginning to feel the dire results of constant war and harassment. General E. S. Canby reported that "the Zuni Indians, partly from the drought of last summer but more from the interruption of their labors by the hostilities of the Navajos are now in a state of great destitution, many of them of absolute suffering from the want of food." He went on to point out the injustice of the situation: "These people have always, I believe, been faithful and they have recently been extremely useful responding promptly to all applications that were made to them, and entering heartily into the plans for the pacification of the Navajos. They are eminently entitled to some consideration." Seeing that the Indian department was being lax in its obligations, Canby continued, "If the Indian Department is provided with the means of affording them any relief, I respectfully request that the attention of the proper authorities may be called to this subject. Corn and wheat for seed would be of great service to them if no other assistance can be furnished."[220]

Governor Pino pressed Canby for this assistance, but there is no record that he received any—a strong indictment, in itself, against the efficacy of government policy in the territory. The Zunis, who had fed the U.S. army, housed American immigrants, fought side by side with the troops, and taken every opportunity to make peace and friendship with the new occupying force in the Southwest were now starving because of what they had given. Instead of storing excess produce, they had traded it to the army. Instead of organizing more military expeditions, they had followed the army's advice and pursued more sedentary endeavors. Now these people were starving because of that army's inability or reluctance (because of priorities) to protect the Pueblo Indians— people who had received at least some protection from the Navajos under Spanish and Mexican rule and whom the United States had promised to protect.

After preliminary councils with Navajo leaders, yet another treaty was signed on February 18, 1861. Though more Navajo headmen signed this agreement than any previous one, the treaty was one of the worst made with the Navajos. After the treaty was signed, and it became apparent that the Civil War was about to break out, the army abandoned Fort Defiance. (With the outbreak of further Navajo hostilities, Fort Canby was founded nearby the following year). Matters worsened in 1861, when, on September 13, the command at Fort Fauntleroy massacred at least ten Navajos gathered for a horse race, including women and children. The stage was set for the final battles, but before they could take place, the Civil War interrupted.[221]

What fighting did take place between the North and South forces in New Mexico was mainly over by 1863, though the Civil War continued to rage elsewhere. The Union forces had some Indian allies, and Pino later reported that he had fought on the North's side during the conflict. A note from General Canby to

Governor Pino on January 15, 1861, tended to corroborate his claim. Canby wrote that "in my intercourse and acquaintance with this man, Juan [Pedro] Pino, I have found him entirely reliable and worthy of any confidence that may be confided in him."[222] Quite a compliment to an Indian leader from an army general.

Frank Hamilton Cushing reported that

> during the early days of the Navajo wars and the subsequent War of Rebellion, he [Pino] was promised, in reward for his services to our Government in both those enterprises, by the Commanding General then stationed at Santa Fe, opportunity for visiting the reverenced home of Washington, or of our Government. Through the intercession of brother priests, however, he was induced, on account of his connection with some religious ceremonials then to take place, to renounce the opportunity.[223]

The agreement reached in 1861 between the Navajos and the United States provided that all Navajos found either to the south or east of Zuni should be treated as robbers. It was also noted that the people of Zuni were to be strictly protected by the United States forces. But 1862 reports indicate that the Navajos regarded the army presence not as an obstacle but a buffer between them and their enemies to the south.[224]

Although the Civil War decreased the number of written and published reports regarding the Pueblo Indians in New Mexico, it did prompt some action toward their enemies. With Navajo depredations continuing and fierce fighting occupying the eastern states, the military in New Mexico did not want to rest. With no Civil War to occupy him in the territory, Colonel James H. Carleton lost patience and decided it was time to end Apache and Navajo depredations once and for all.

There would be no more talk or treaties. The fierce and brutal roundup of Navajos under Kit Carson began in 1863. The campaign was vicious. Under military orders, Zunis joined the army as allies in the preliminary engagements, perhaps going out on expeditions headed by Albert Pfeiffer, who was leading vengeful Ute parties against the Navajos while acting as agent to the Utes. Cushing reported that the Zunis signed a treaty with Pfeiffer, which was perhaps a reference to joint raids. In any event, Pfeiffer did deal with Governor Pino and in October of 1863 gave him a Mississippi rifle and twenty rounds of ammunition with which "to defend himself and family."[225] During the latter months of 1863, the Zunis joined Carson in raids into the Navajo heartland. In August 1863, Zunis captured thirty-five head of cattle and one horse. Reports indicate that by September of that year, the Zunis' campaign had resulted in Navajo deaths as well. Twenty-three Zunis went out with Carson in September, capturing about fifty head of sheep and goats before returning home. In October of 1863, the Zunis celebrated a scalp dance at the pueblo, hanging Navajo scalps from the pole.[226]

Feelings at Zuni seemed to change as the campaign continued. Though initially the Zunis joined Carson in his slash-and-burn rampage, it soon became evident that the army did not discriminate in its practices. There are indications that Zuni fields were burned, and Zuni people may have been victimized. One patrol destroyed corn within Zuni territory, and another burned forty thousand pounds of what may have been Zuni wheat.[227]

The Zunis had long known what the army had yet to learn: The Navajos were made up of hundreds of small bands, and no single leader directed all the people. Pino and the Zunis had allowed small groups of Navajos to settle within the tribe's boundaries and continued, even during the war, to trade with some Navajos and Apaches. Now, as the United States launched its nearly genocidal attack on the Navajo people, the army began to hear irritating reports that their old allies, the Zunis, were harboring Navajo refugees.

Some of these reports indicated that Navajos were hiding near Rito Quemado, to the south of Zuni, but expeditions to the area verified that "scouts have already gone to that place from here and traveled the whole length and breadth of the creek and have not been able to find any of those Rancherias nor have they been able to see Indians in any large numbers until they crossed the Colorado Chiquito."[228] Evidently the army was finding that all of Zuni territory was still free of intruders. But there was one place they had not searched.

Carleton and Carson paid no attention whatever to any previous treaties—the Navajos had only two choices: be exterminated or surrender unconditionally. Groups of Navajos who had lived by the treaties or settled permanently and begun agricultural pursuits were not exempt from the army's wrath. There is every indication that the Zunis did not approve of the army's methods. There were reports in 1864 that Navajos attempting to avoid Bosque Redondo (the concentration camp set up for Navajos on the Pecos River) were being hidden in the Zuni Pueblo itself. When Zunis were questioned, during a short truce in the war, a United States officer reported that

> there are in their town, many Navajos, mostly ricos, who are hiding there. I do not wish to take the responsibility of attacking them during the existing truce, and I am unable to dispose of them properly if I take them prisoners; yet, they are, as the Zunis say, unwilling to go to the Bosque Redondo and I have therefore thought it my duty to give Major Eaton notice of these facts, that he may be enabled to take whatever action he may deem proper in the premises.[229]

In July of that year, Eaton did send a message to Governor Pino, warning the Zunis not to harbor any Navajo refugees.[230] Then in August, apparently unsatisfied with the results of his warning, he visited the pueblo and left Governor Pino to ponder this written order:

> Visited this pueblo for the purpose of impressing upon the minds of these Indians the necessity of their not advising or aiding in any manner the Navajos or Apache Indians. Either with grain or eatables of any kind. Powder, lead, or arms nor allow them in their pueblo, but advise them to go to their reservation at the Bosque Redondo on the Pecos River. By pursuing this policy, they will retain the good will of the U.S. Government; otherwise, it will be necessary to chastise them.[231]

The situation eventually led to the arrest of José Maria, who had been the principal guide for the army in a number of campaigns against the Navajos and now was apparently viewed as a traitor. He was apprehended at Zuni and imprisoned at Fort Wingate for trading with Apaches. Governor Pino was able to obtain José Maria's release into his custody within a month of the arrest, but it must have made an indelible impression on both men, who had spent the past two decades fighting side by side with the United States. Pino, who was seventy years old or more at the time, would see the army invade the pueblo the next month. In October more than one hundred Navajos were arrested inside the Zuni Pueblo and taken to Fort Wingate for transportation to Bosque Redondo.[232]

It was a time of terrible hardship for the Zunis. On top of the fact that the military engagements were destroying Zuni crops and had completely curtailed trade at the pueblo, in 1864 a devastating drought struck the area. It was so severe that in April 1865 the Zunis' Indian agent reported that their crops had failed for the two previous years. Despite all these hardships, Pino's correspondence shows that he and the tribe continued to feed and house exploring expeditions and other whites who came their way.[233]

By 1865 it is likely that all of the Navajos who were at peace with Zuni, the sedentary bands, had been gathered up and sent on the Long Walk (Hwalte in Navajo) to Bosque Redondo. The Zunis rejoined the United States forces in the fight against the remaining resistance. Several large expeditions took place. In mid-1865 the commander of Fort Wingate reported that Antonio Mejicano and two other citizens of Cubero had applied for and received permission to make a campaign against the Navajos,[234] together with seventy-five to one hundred Zunis.[235] Later in that same month of May, Mejicano and the expedition returned, "reporting 21 killed and 5 women prisoners." He also stated that some of the Navajos they had killed were "nearly destitute of everything" and were surviving on pine nuts.[236] The army gave Mejicano permission to continue his raids and report the results.

Later the same year, in August of 1865, a Zuni war party killed several prominent Navajos during a battle on the northwest boundary of Zuni land, the Rio Puerco of the West. Governor Pino sent war chief José Maria to Fort Wingate to report the results of that battle to the commandant. Maria stated that the Zunis had overcome a party of twenty-five to thirty Navajos and killed "Navajo

Blanco and wife, Barboncito Negro, and the son of Capitan Largo, Diego . . . from the Reservation and captured 7 horses, 2 Colt revolvers, 12 setts [*sic*] of Bows and arrows, many saddles and blankets, bridles, etc., about 12 pds. of gunpowder, etc. One Zuni Ind. was killed, named Weiyman . . ."[237] When José Maria asked if the Zunis could again take the field against the Navajos, the post commander responded that they should and he would provide them with ammunition. During the same month, two Navajos who came near Ojo Caliente, the Zuni farming village, were killed by the Zunis.[238]

There were more indications of joint Ute/Zuni war parties against the Navajos in both 1865 and 1866. In May of 1865, there were reports that Zunis, Utes, and others had attacked Navajos on their way to Fort Sumner, even though they were accompanied by escorts. Old grievances against the Navajos evidently prompted their enemies to take advantage of the situation. Conditions at Fort Sumner were causing daily deaths, but the situation in the Navajo homeland was far worse. The Navajos were finally being soundly defeated.[239]

In 1866 Zuni's governor presented himself at Santa Fe to ask permission to take the field against the Navajos again. He reported that twenty-five Zunis and twelve Utes had just returned from scouting the Navajos and he was ready to go out again, but he hoped to obtain some supplies first. The governor said that if the Zunis were supplied with powder, lead, caps, etc., the pueblo would always have a force in readiness.[240] During the course of 1866, the Zunis captured many Navajos and killed even more during several expeditions against their hard-pressed enemies.[241]

The Zunis also guided cavalry expeditions during the year. One command, under Captain John S. Crouch, went from Ojo Caliente to the Little Colorado. While on the march, the command came across the tracks of three Coyotero Apache ponies. The Zuni guide indicated that the Apaches were on their way to the pueblo to trade—in the midst of the wars, the Zunis were still willing to trade with friends, despite tribal connections. But the Navajos were near the end of their road. Those who were free at this point were reportedly very poor and destitute and feared coming to Fort Wingate to surrender because they would have to travel through either Zuni or Hopi territory. As usual, the cavalry expedition leaders in 1866 left testimonials to the ability and character of Governor Pino.[242]

Because of the Pueblo Indians' alliance with the United States government and the trust earned by such leaders as Pedro Pino; because the government respected the Pueblo way of life, knew how much it was indebted to the Pueblos, militarily and economically, and recognized how important these Indians were to American colonization (or colonialization, depending on your perspective) of the Southwest, during this period of turmoil, President Abraham Lincoln presented the Indian pueblos with a symbolic gift that is remembered in every Pueblo community in New Mexico today. President Lincoln sent Zuni governor Pino and the other Pueblo governors in New Mexico silver-handled canes as symbols of the authority of their office. The king of Spain had given the Pueblo leaders similar canes years before, and, in fact, some pueblos today have not only the Lincoln canes but the Spanish ones which preceded them. They are all passed from leader to leader as a symbol of the sovereignty and power of his office.[243]

As more and more whites, for one reason or another, passed through Zuni territory, Pino and the Zunis cemented their reputation for hospitality, despite the ongoing Navajo conflicts. As early as 1859, a mail route through Zuni to California had been explored. By 1865 a system of mail delivery was developing in the Southwest, with one route linking Albuquerque and Prescott, Arizona. Albert Banta was one of the men who contracted to deliver the mail over that route,[244] which passed through Zuni and which Pino began to use to enhance his communication with U.S. officials. Banta was snowed in at Zuni during the winter of 1866, and the Zunis housed and fed him congenially, even though he reported that during that year there was a severe epidemic and the Zunis "died off like sheep with the rot."[245]

Despite the hardships the Zunis were going through, when Banta himself became ill, the people cared for him for more than two weeks and eventually adopted him into the tribe. After inadvertently disobeying a Zuni rule during a religious observance (evidently Deshkwi), Banta became very sick.[246] After he had been delirious for some time, Governor Pino joined the *caciques* in

Banta's room and examined him.²⁴⁷ The Zunis had a long discussion in their native tongue, and then Governor Pino turned to
Banta (who reported that Pino spoke "very good Spanish") and
said, "We have been talking about you; you have been sick a long
time but are going to get well now, but on condition that you
become a Zuni. The Great Spirit says you ate meat thru ignorance,
but by becoming a Zuni and complying with our rules and rites
you will recover. Can you do this?"

"Of course," answered Banta.

"Your Zuni name is now Too-loosh-too-loo," Pino told him.
Then Pino and the Zuni religious leaders shook Banta's hand and
filed out.²⁴⁸

Banta reported that

> sometime after this some of my Apache friends—Chief Escopah
> and ten or twelve of his men—came along and hearing I was in
> the village they came to see me. I told the Chief if he and his
> people would help me on and off my mule I would go in to
> Wingate with them. But before leaving, the Zunis held a coun
> cil with the Apaches at which the Apaches were told that I was a
> Zuni, and if any harm came to me, the Zunis would hold them
> responsible, and that not one of them would return home alive.
> The Apache Chief said in reply that I was his friend and broth
> er and they need not fear on that account. ²⁴⁹

Though he recovered fully, Banta said he was not well for
eight full months.

Banta made interesting comments on Zuni/Apache and
Zuni/Navajo relations, reporting aspects of Zuni politics which
Governor Pino was constantly charged with maintaining. Banta
described the system of trade which was going on with the
Apaches. He said the two tribes met at the southwest boundary of
Zuni's territory, the Little Colorado. "The Little Colorado," Banta
said, "has always been 'neutral ground.'" A system of signals preceded such trading. "One time the Apaches had signaled from the
summit of the Mogollons [of their] intention to meet the Zunis on
the river to trade. Quite a large party of us went down there to
meet them. Our party camped on the north side of the river and
the Apaches on the south side. Nevertheless and notwithstanding

the 'peace treaty,' we were armed and ready for any emergency."²⁵⁰

Still, Zuni/Navajo relations were not good, and that troubled Governor Pino. Banta mentions several instances of Navajo conflicts during the period he was at the pueblo (mainly between 1865 and 1879). He also claimed that he was asked by the Zuni leaders to become the tribe's war captain. "But I declined that honor; nevertheless, I went with them against the thieving Navajos on several occasions."²⁵¹

Banta's description of the Zunis' hospitality merits repeating:

> The Zunis were the best people in the world; they were honest and truthful, and were the most hospitable people living. No matter what house you may enter, nor how many during the day, you are politely asked to "eemoo" (take a seat), and the woman immediately sets before you something to eat with a request . . . (please to eat), and this is done to anyone entering a house. It is a religious rite with them, and you are expected to take at least a bite, if no more, after which you may say, "ellah-quah" (thank you) . . . .²⁵²

Much has been written about the final days of the Navajo wars. Many Navajos died because of the United States' policy, a policy which no one can be proud of today. During the Civil War, Congress realized that Indian matters were being ignored and promised to turn its attention to some of these problems when war concluded. In 1867 the Indian Peace Commission was formed, and it promptly recommended that a new treaty be negotiated with the Navajos. It was admitted that the Bosque Redondo experiment was not a success despite the fact that it had helped end hostilities. With the enactment of a new treaty with the Navajos in 1868, the tribe was allowed to leave Fort Sumner and return to northwest New Mexico.

Even before the end of the war, tensions began to ease somewhat in the Zuni area, as evidenced by the number of whites like Banta who began to appear at the pueblo. An undetermined number of Navajos had been able to escape the Bosque Redondo ordeal by hiding in the mountains or canyons, but eighty-five hundred had been taken to Fort Sumner, and the experience was enough to end much of the Navajo raiding which had been going on for centuries.[253] Pino's work in fighting off the raiding Navajos was not over, however. Occasional raids continued after 1867, some of them serious, and there was also a continuing threat from marauding Apache bands, which preyed on Zuni for many years to come.

Although Pino must certainly have been happy about the pacification of the Navajos, he must also have wondered about the way it was accomplished and the settlement the Navajos received. The reservation set aside for them totaled four million acres. By 1911 it would grow to twelve million acres by additional executive orders. This was far more territory than the tribe had ever controlled previous to the 1868 treaty. Pino, on the other hand, for all his efforts on behalf of the U.S. government had been ignored. Unless the government needed corn, additional soldiers, or guides, Zuni was left to fare for itself. Little effort had been made to set aside the Zunis' land, though Pino still believed the United States' promise that it would faithfully guarantee the tribe's land and protect its rights.[254] Thus far, Pino and the Zunis had been able to protect their boundaries themselves, but with the pacification of the Navajos, greater and more subtle competition for the Zunis' land would begin to develop. Disease was still whittling away at the population of the Zunis, further reducing their defensive capabilities. Though he was now more than seventy years old, Pedro Pino's work was far from over.

seven
Expeditions to and from Zuni: "Enough to Pay Them for Going"

The controversy over Pueblo Indian land grants and citizenship was building in 1868. The commissioner of Indian affairs reported optimistically that most of the grants to the pueblos had been confirmed and the rest should be verified soon.[255] On the other hand, the Santa Fe Ring controlled New Mexico. None of the land grants bought and illegally enlarged by the ring were near Zuni, but another method the group was initiating to wrestle land from the pueblos affected Zuni relations. The ring was trying to establish the Pueblo Indians as citizens. On the surface, this sounded like an honorable idea to many people (except most of the Indians), but the real objective was to remove Pueblo Indian land from its trust status. Then it could be alienated through legal channels which the Indians did not understand (only the ring's attorneys understood the "legal channels" in New Mexico in those days). The end result was Pueblo land falling into the hands of land-speculating Anglos. In 1868 the special agent for the Pueblos reported that Stephen Benton Elkins was interested in the movement to grant the Indians citizenship. "Smooth Steve" Elkins was one of the principals in the Santa Fe Ring.[256]

With land grants a topic of special interest in New Mexico in 1868, renewing pressure on Pueblo lands, the Zunis traveled to Fort Wingate and applied for protection for Nutria Springs.[257] No action was taken, but the movement to allow alienation of Pueblo land resulted in the Slough decision in 1869. Chief Justice Slough of the New Mexico Territory put the Pueblos on "equal" footing as citizens with his decision (they were not allowed to vote, however). The agent to the Pueblos complained that the Indians did not want this status and should be treated specially by Congress.[258]

Pino sensed more and more pressure on the Zuni people. The agent had made a few telling comments the previous year: "These Indians, as you can readily imagine, are fully aware that every year something is done by the government towards relieving the wants of other Indians while at the same time they see that *nothing* is done for them towards relieving their wants, not even so far as to comply with some of the many promises which from time to time have been made to them."[259] He elaborated in his 1869 report: "As the department is doubtless aware, no appropriation has been made for these Indians since 1856; and until within the last few days they have received no presents of agricultural implements & etc. since 1857."[260]

A small insight into the equal-minded philosophy of Pueblo culture can be gained from the agent's report for the following year. "Last spring," he wrote,

> I received a few agricultural implements for the Pueblos, which I proceeded to distribute to the different villages, according to the population. The amount was not near enough to supply all, and, as a consequence, when the proportions alluded to were offered to the Pueblos of Tersuque [*sic*], Pojuaque, Nambi, San Ildefonso, and San Juan, they refused to receive them, saying that if every person could not receive something, they would take none at all. . . .[261]

In 1869 Pino led two delegations on pilgrimages. In July the Zunis heard of the approaching eclipse of the sun and traveled to Fort Wingate to learn details. Undoubtedly the *bekwinne,* or sun priest, was much interested in the event, which was predicted to take place on August 7. The group visited the fort on July 26 and asked for information. A. W. Evans, commander at Wingate, reported,

> . . . *Pedro Pino,* or *Laia-à-et-tsalòu*—a leading man of *Zuni,* formerly Governor, now *Ayudanté de los Caciques de Zuni,* has visited this post to enquire about the eclipse of the sun of August 7, 1869, of which he has heard. He is, like all the people of Zuni,

a good man—friendly, peace-able [*sic*], and always to be trusted. He is recommended to the good treatment of all Americans who may meet him.

His companions on his visit here are: Ouatchiufuino, principal Cacique; Manuel Ouacamañix, second Cacique; Patricio Pino, Son of Pedro Pino [Ba:lawadiwa] Juan José; Lucero; and Jose L´nicio.[262]

Albert Banta, who was at the pueblo during this period, recalled the eclipse, though he may have embellished his memory slightly:

I remember one time on returning from Santa Fe, where I had gone to purchase a few goods for trade, I had no sooner returned to the village when suddenly a "wailing" started all over the village. Asking the cause of the monotonous wailing I was answered by the question, "Is it true the sun is going to die?" I replied, "Of course not, what gave you such a notion?" They said an American had been there while I was gone and said that on a certain day the sun would die, and if it did all would die as the sun is the Father of all life. It struck me the American had refference [*sic*] to an eclipse; looking at an old almanac I saw that an eclipse of the sun was due in August, a few days hence, I explained the matter to them by illustration of just how it would be and the result; that if cloudy, it would hardly be noticed at all. Immediately one of the men rushed out and reaching the top of the highest house announced to the people what I had said, the wailing as suddenly ceased as it had begun . . . .[263]

The second pilgrimage that Pino took was the result of continued Navajo depredations on the pueblo. On November 11, 1869, the *Weekly New Mexican* reported that on the fourth of November,

. . . a delegation of sixty-five Indians from the Pueblo of Zuni arrived in the city [of Santa Fe] and proceeded in a body to [the] United States Indian Superintendency, halted and grouped in front of which and . . . they presented an interesting appearance. Last night they encamped in the city near the state house, and will today or tomorrow . . . seek and obtain a formal interview with Major Clinton, the Superintendent. The delegation has come accompanied by the governor of the Pueblo; and we learn the object of the visit is in connection with alleged recent depredations committed on life and property at Zuni by the Navajos, and in connection the relations of threatened hostility subsisting between the Zunis and Navajos.[264]

The government did nothing, and in the following year, Pedro Pino, who must have been nearing eighty years of age, went out with a war party against the Navajos. On April 17, 1870, an officer at Fort Wingate reported that Pedro Pino "has been at this post for 2 days resting after a scout after a party of Navajos who had stolen stock from his people."[265]

W. F. M. Arny, a special agent, visited Zuni and talked to the leaders in 1870. Pino articulated the grievances of the Zunis. "They complained," Arny noted, "that 'no agent had visited them for ten years.' That 'last October they went to Santa Fe, and did not get enough to pay them for going.' 'They begin to think that because they do not steal, the Government does not give them anything.' They begin to think that 'if they steal like the Navajos, they would get something,'" Evidently the topic of a title for the Zunis' land came up during the conversations with Pino because Arny commented, "These Indians have no title to their land. A law of Congress establishing a reservation where they are, and to give them a title to a sufficient amount of land for their subsistence [should be enacted] . . . There are no citizens living near them and none within forty miles."[266]

Arny left a testimonial with Governor Pino before leaving the pueblo, concurring with Major William Redwood Price's assessment of Pino and the Zunis. "He represents a flourishing industrious agricultural people who should be treated with justly by all parties passing through the country they occupy."[267] Pino was attempting to document the Zunis' goodwill and keep a record of the United States/Zuni contact by requesting and collecting these testimonials. He was successful in doing this, and as a result we can verify the observations of men like Banta, as well as document the veracity of Pino's statements, particularly his description of Zuni boundaries and the history of Zuni's political turmoil over them.[268]

Testimonials about Governor Pino and the Zunis came from two other people during 1869. On July 12, C. E. Cooley and Henry Dodd visited the pueblo from new Fort Wingate. They intended to go on an expedition to locate a lost gold mine they had heard was beyond Zuni territory. Cooley and Dodd served as guides and scouts for the army and are credited with naming Showlow, Arizona. On leaving the Zuni villages, the two left a note with Pedro Pino. "I take great pleasure," they wrote, "in testifying to the good qualities, kindness & hospitality of the Govonor [*sic*] & the Indians of Zuni in general—they received us like brothers & treated us with the utmost kindness giving us everything their town could aford [*sic*]—may they ever be prosperous & happy is the sincere wish of their friends."[269]

Others who left testimonials with Governor Pino during 1870 included John S. A. Clark and John H. Farrand, who said they were received and "treated with the utmost kindness & hospitality" by the Zuni statesman. They recommended him to all those who might pass through the Zuni villages.[270]

With the Navajos' new reservation including land that they had never previously controlled—land which had once belonged to Zunis, Hopis, Southern Utes, and Southern Paiutes—some in the government understood that an injustice was taking place. The Board of Indian Commissioners, which was formed in 1869, was aware of the "apparent inconsistency of expending government funds on the warlike and largely ignoring the peaceful groups"[271] but claimed that the expenditures were necessary to keep those tribes peaceful and secure their continued existence.

Arny suggested that a reservation be set aside for the Zunis, recommending that it should consist of "a tract of land thirty miles square," with the central village at the heart. He also recommended that the Zunis' proposed reservation be surveyed at government expense so that the Indians could tell what land was actually theirs.[272] In reality Arny was taking a great deal of land away from Zuni. If the Zunis had been limited to an area thirty miles square, they would have lost the majority of their territory. But Arny's recommendation was not acted upon.

Navajo/Zuni hostilities forced Arny to visit Zuni again in the spring of 1871. Navajos had killed two Zunis, and the Zunis in retaliation had killed two Navajos. Arny reported that there "were various cases of murder and robbery between these two tribes" but made the claim "[I] succeeded, I trust, in making a lasting peace between them."[273] All property was reportedly restored to its original owners.

In the meantime, the military was seemingly taking a position of letting the Navajos and Zunis fight it out. In 1870 General John Pope, commander of the Department of the Missouri, made these revealing comments: "I do not believe that Fort Wingate is necessary . . . . The Navajos are peaceable, and likely, I think to remain so. Any evil acts they do are simple robberies of sheep or mules, and once in a long time the killing of a herder." He concluded that it was too expensive to keep the fort in operation.[274]

In fact, the army did not take seriously any depredations against the Zunis by the Navajos. If there were no depredations against the white settlements, the army was satisfied. Banta reported that "at this time—May, 1870—there was not a settlement or single soul to be met with from the time I left Zuni until I reached Bob Postle's ranch in Chino Valley—twenty-five miles east of Prescott."[275] The Zunis had been severely reduced in numbers and, indeed, needed the protection of the army. The government, however, was not in the business of providing the same kind of protection for Indian tribes as it offered to white businessmen.

Pino's problems in 1871 were not limited to Navajo depredations. In Arny's report for that year, he discussed the case of a trader, Sol Barth, who had been convicted of improper activities.[276] His goods had been entrusted to Pino, but the Zuni governor had had enough dealings with the government to know that if he kept the goods, he might, at some future date, be charged with stealing them. As the government did not seem to have a very good memory, he turned the goods over to the military authorities to be safe. The agent, who declared that Zuni was "a good place for traders who sell whiskey and gunpowder to the Southern Apache Indians," decided that henceforth no traders would be allowed at Zuni.[277] This was a severe restriction on the Zunis and a complete departure from the policy followed ever since Backus had ordered corn from Zuni while building Fort Defiance. Zuni had been a trade center for hundreds of years. The tribe's land was in jeopardy, their trade was now being restricted, and to make matters even worse, the military was beginning to cultivate its own corn on what had once been Indian land.

Navajo hostilities culminated in a conflict with Zuni in 1873. The Zunis battled the Navajos on the border of their land, the Rio Puerco of the West. The fight claimed at least thirty Navajos and fifteen Zunis. This was the last major violent conflict between the two tribes.[278] The Zunis had apparently repelled the Navajos' every attempt to breach their borders. But what the Navajos could not do, the U.S. federal government would accomplish during the next six years.

Timothy O'Sullivan, the famous early western photographer, happened to document a war dance during 1873. This remarkable photograph shows spears, muskets, and rifles in the hands of Zuni men evidently dancing in anticipation of this battle with the Navajos.[279]

O'Sullivan was leading one of the surveying parties in the Wheeler expedition. Lieutenant George M. Wheeler's geographical expedition provided the first detailed maps of the area surrounding the pueblo of Zuni. Using the best guides, including Albert Banta and a Zuni named Swzano, the party crisscrossed the area to make the survey. Pino understood it was a surveying and mapping expedition and went to great pains to explain Zuni boundaries to the men, as well as assist the project in any way he could.

Francis Klett was in charge of another of Wheeler's parties, which arrived at Zuni Pueblo on July 22, 1873, and was met by Governor Pino. Klett reported the conversations that followed: "The executive authority of the Zuni is vested in an officer styled governor—one Pedro Pino—who, however is but the mouth-piece of the spiritual ruler, the cacique." Klett is correct about the final authority of the *caciques* (there were more than one), but as mentioned earlier, Pino's authority would not be interfered with except in extreme cases. "The orders of the latter," Klett continued, "are the laws governing the tribe, their execution simply resting with the governor." [280]

Klett described Pino as being "of commanding presence and affable manners; his hair is snow-white. He told us he had been governor of the Zuni people for many years, and that the tribe had always been friendly to the whites (Americans), from whom he had many testimonials to the latter effect." Klett provides the reader with a detailed description of the way Governor Pino worked: how he met new representatives of the United States, explained his impression of these representatives, immediately reassured them about the Zunis' alliance with the federal government, and then later discussed policy, emphasizing approaches to problems with each group. To demonstrate his continuing friendship with the U.S. government, Pedro Pino ordered his son Patricio to "bring him certain papers. He produced letters from officers of our army and private citizens, which referred to the governor in the highest terms and also spoke of his uniform kindness in their treatment of his people."[281]

"The Americans," continued Governor Pino,

> treat us well, but the Mexicans very badly; the latter have always maltreated us, and we want them neither to go through our country nor to reside among us. The heavens punish us by long drought for allowing them to remain on the Colorado Chiquito. My cacique, who prays for rain, and who is the spiritual and temporal ruler of this people, watches the sun daily, and is much distressed because no rain falls.[282]

Pino went on to say that his tribe had always owned its land and now he wanted from the United States government a "perpetual title to the Zuni country, which had been handed down to us by our forefathers, through all time. We are peaceable and do not make war; if we have a title to our lands from the Great Father, we can show the document, and even the Mexican will respect it. The *cacique* who was present nodded in assent. . . ." The presence of the *cacique* underlines the reliability and importance of what Pino had to say. The old governor again described the boundaries of Zuni land: "the country between the Neutrias [Nutria Springs] and colorado Chiquito [Little Colorado], some sixty miles, and Agua Fria [spring in the Zuni Mountains] and the Moquis [Hopi] settlements, about one hundred miles apart."[283]

The Zunis had suffered through literally centuries of religious persecution at the hands of the Catholic Spanish and Mexican governments. That persecution resulted in a strong prejudice against Hispanos (Mexicans) by Pino and the Zunis, a prejudice hard to erase even today. Though Pino had his political reasons for allying with the United States, his commitment to U.S. policy and hostility toward former Spanish practices may have been somewhat misplaced. Nevertheless, he was dealing with a nearly all-powerful entity in the United States of 1872, and he made his points with strength.

Pino said that his *caciques* especially resented the presence of the Mexicans who were now encroaching upon Zuni land. Then he allowed Klett to view a dance and said, "No Mexican shall ever look upon the performance of this holy and sacred rite. The Americans have ever been our friends, and are good and excellent people."[284] If O'Sullivan's photograph pictures this dance, then Pino's description of it as a rain dance may be further evidence of his diplomacy.

The governor continued that there was a Mexican at Ojo de Benado (south of Zuni) and another on the Little Colorado. "The Cacique of my nation is very sorry on this account and the rain will not fall while these wicked men inhabit our territory. I will deem it a special favor if you will intercede with the Great Father for a title for us to our country: this will satisfy us. You men are good, have seen the sacred dance . . . and we shall have rain." Following the rain dance, Klett reported, "It may be a fact of importance to the superstitious to know that it *did* rain that evening, and most heavily, the storm lasting several hours!"[285]

Klett added his note to the papers kept fastidiously by Pino: "The people were very kind and considerate," he wrote, "and have done all in their power to make our state as pleasant and agreeable as possible, they have given us an opportunity to witness the religious ceremony of the cachina, and given us every chance to observe their peculiar customs and the ways of their every day life."[286]

The following month, on August 6, 1873, Wheeler himself arrived at Zuni Pueblo. He reported that he had "careful conversation" with the governor, with one important topic again being Zuni land. "The grant from the Spaniards, or rather the Mexicans as asserted by Pedro Pino," Wheeler wrote, "covers the following area: bounded on the north by the dividing ridge between Zuni River and the Puerco, on the east by the summit of the Zuni Mountains, on the south by an east west line through the Salt Lake, and on the West by the Little Colorado." Wheeler also mentioned some of the Zuni ruins throughout the area which he had visited or knew of: "Three other pueblos found to be, one at Ojo Benado, a second a short distance to the south and east, a third at Tule Spring, now in ruins, were once inhabited."[287]

Wheeler also left a testimonial with Pino, written on September 1, 1973, praising the old man but with a final condescending qualification so typical of the period. "This is to certify," Wheeler wrote, "that Pedro Pino, Governor of the Zuni Indians has been very kind and accommodating to all the parties, connected with the expedition of 1873: has cheerfully furnished any desired information, and is evidently a man of more than ordinary intelligence for one of his race."[288]

It is important that both Wheeler and Klett reported a description of the area which the Zunis inhabited and claimed, and it is also a testimony to Pino's efforts at explaining Zuni rights. It seems incongruous, however, that Wheeler later commented that all the Pueblo Indians' titles vested their lands to them permanently "except, perhaps, for the Moquis and Zuni."[289] This statement becomes clearer when we learn that Wheeler took advice from Smooth Steve Elkins of the Santa Fe Ring on New Mexican land.[290]

The Zunis had now been allied with the United States for almost three decades under Pino. They had supplied feed corn, supplies, and housing for all Americans who came through their land. They had guided exploring parties. Finally in 1873, following Wheeler's departure, Pino was appointed United States forage agent for the area, supposedly guaranteeing the payment for feed which Pino supplied to official parties passing through Zuni territory.[291]

eight
"Our Sheep Is Dying!"

In the latter half of the 1870s, Pedro Pino would begin to lose the battle which he had been fighting for decades. By the end of the decade, the Zunis would lose approximately 75 percent of their land and many of their rights. Pino had nurtured goodwill for the United States and an alliance with its army. But the goodwill of the Zunis was not reciprocated by the United States.

Through the years, Pino and the Zunis had made continual requests for teachers. The Zunis, according to the agent in 1874, were not only willing to have a teacher at the pueblo but had repeatedly asked for one.[292] In December of that year, Indian Agent Ben Thomas announced he had hired a teacher, William Burgess, for Zuni.[293] The Zunis would soon learn that a "teacher" from the Anglo nation was not quite the same as a Pueblo one. The government objective for the teacher was more to convert than to teach, to change the Indian children, to turn the people away from their own religion, and to help *control* the tribe through cultural conditioning. The "free enterprise" system was also responsible for the appointment of another trader at Zuni in 1874, William Wallace, who received his license in November.[294]

With these new whites at Zuni, the agent was to write official letters not to Governor Pino but to teacher Burgess. When he feared that pressures were building against Zuni land, Thomas did write to Burgess. Pino had been meeting with Thomas regarding Zuni land in 1875, and the agent wrote to Burgess in March, saying that "I have been talking a good deal with the Indians, but they do not feel authorized to do as I advise. It is *very important* for them to file their land grant in the Surveyor General's Office, so that steps may be taken to have it confirmed by Congress." Thomas noted that Governor Pino was very careful with the papers in his possession. "They want to take it [the grant] home with them to be sent back directly, with other papers, by the Governor." And Thomas must have given a severe shock to Governor Pino when he suggested that "this land grant only entitles them to one league each way from the Pueblo of Zuni. If they have other land titles, be sure that the Governor brings them with him when he comes."[295] Thomas went on to explain that Governor Pino had no authority to expel trespassers who were outside the limits of this grant.

Though Thomas said he knew of only one Zuni land grant in this letter to the teacher, in his annual report to the commissioner of Indian affairs for 1875, he stated that "the Indians have hitherto succeeded in raising enough for their subsistence by planting every season three different farming districts [296] outside the limits of their *land-grants*, which they claim as their own . . . ."[297] Thomas would certainly have learned the boundaries of Zuni land from Pino, but he did not mention them.

During 1875 a bill was enacted by Congress funding a survey of the new territorial line between New Mexico and Arizona. The government notified Pino and requested that he supply two guides for the surveying party, as well as provide the party with enough hay and grain to feed seven hundred mules and horses.[298] Throughout August Major Chandler Robbins surveyed the arbitrary line where it cut through Zuni lands.[299] It is ironic that this party, which the Zunis guided, supplied with food, and were instrumental in making successful, was indirectly responsible for the loss of a great deal of their land. All of the land on the Arizona side of the line was now in jeopardy and would eventually be lost to the tribe.

Pino still exerted control over his people's traditional boundaries and had authority over the land the Zunis owned. His trading activities took him to the southwestern boundaries in 1875, where he delivered large amounts of corn to the influential New Mexican merchant Juan Christobal Armijo. Octogenarian Pino traded the corn for brown sugar when they met on the Little Colorado.[300] The longtime merchants in the territory still knew who controlled which territory and was profitable to trade with.

Pino also traveled to Santa Fe, probably in 1875, to deliver the Zunis' grant to Indian Agent Thomas. On July 13 Thomas sent a copy back to the Zuni *alcalde* (officer of the law).[301] Shortly afterward, in 1876, Pino complained by letter that there was trespassing on Zuni land. Thomas replied, "I have been informed by letter that the people of Zuni are troubled by large flocks of Mexican sheep being brought into the limits of what you call your country; that these sheep consume all the grass that your flocks should properly have . . . . I went to the Surveyor General's office to see your original grant from the Mexican Government."[302] Thomas then reported that the pueblo, by the terms of the grant, was entitled to four square leagues—roughly thirty-six square miles. "You have as much right," Thomas told Pino, "to the adjacent grazing country belonging to the Government of the United States with your flocks, no one has any right to drive you away, and you must not submit to be driven away. *All the other land,* you have no right to drive anyone away from who has first possession."[303]

The elder Zuni statesman was shocked to learn of this interpretation, but as yet, all was not lost. The Zunis still owned their land and could use all that was theirs traditionally according to one interpretation of Thomas's confusing letter. And Thomas knew that the Zunis could not live on four square leagues.[304] Pino still hoped that his efforts would be successful, and he continued to treat all newcomers with the same kindness and hospitality. H. C. Hodge, an attorney and correspondent for the *San Francisco Chronicle* and *Detroit Free Press,* visited Zuni and commented, with the same alacrity as many before him, that "my visit to the Zunis has been pleasant. They are true friends of the whites and ever have been."[305]

In 1876 Mormon missionaries arrived in Zuni territory. On April 2, Ammon Tenney and Robert H. Smith reached Ojo Pescado. The previous night they had camped in the Zuni Mountains, and when they got to the village, they had only bread. When the Zunis discovered the Mormons had no food, they fed them and then began to talk. The two missionaries visited and talked with the civil authorities of the main Zuni village and farming villages, with military leaders, and with religious officials. They were housed one night in the home of a *cacique* at Ojo Caliente, where the missionaries helped to repair dams built by the Zunis.[306]

The Zunis, including Pino, complained bitterly to Smith and Tenney about the recent attitude of the government:

> Many of the leading men said that their fathers had often told them at some time in the future a class of intelligent people would come among them . . . . They stated that a few years ago, when the United States officers came among them to fix the boundaries of their reservation, they thought they were the men spoken of by their fathers, but they soon found that they were not, as they only put them on a small portion of land and told them to stay on it, and then left them.[307]

Pedro Pino went on to tell Tenney that "he was at Santa Fe at the time that each delegation was called" and "got the understanding that" the Zunis' land would be recognized as "from Agua Frio [Fria]—dos Cieros [Sierras]—Salina [Zuni Salt Lake]—Rio Colorado [Little Colorado]—dos mesa-redondo—oho [ojo or spring] Navajo—oho-a-Magre [?]—Rio Puerco—Ciera [Sierra] da [de] Zuni to the place of commencement." Tenney ends his report of Pino's plea with this statement: "Our sheep is dying what shall we do,"[308] which may refer to the missionary's appraisal of his "flock" of potential converts or may be a statement of fact about the Zunis' sheep.

The Mormons were intrigued with the Zunis and, identifying them in relation to the two main groups in the Book of Mormon, believed them to be descendants of the Nephites as opposed to most Indians, who were descendants of the Lamanites. The Zunis lived in towns and wore clothing similar to Americans, and there were a number of albinos at the pueblo. All these characteristics were cited as proof of the Zunis' "civilization," while the albinos suggested to the Mormons that this tribe was blessed by God and returning to a state which was "white and delightsome." Partly because of the Mormons' great interest in the Zunis, settlements were founded in and near Zuni territory. St. Johns is probably in its present location partly because of Wilford Woodruff's interest in the tribe.[309]

Also in 1876 Mormon settlers moved to a site near the present town of Ramah, New Mexico, a few miles to the east of Zuni and on Zuni land. The Zunis allowed them to settle there and sold corn to the Mormons, who, in turn, carried out their proselytizing. It was hard going for the Mormons from the first, and things only got worse. "The flourishing little settlement [Savoia] found a new trial to meet when in the autumn of 1877, about one hundred Mormon converts moved in with them from the southern states . . . ." Most of the party had come from Arkansas. "One of their number, a Thomas West, had stopped in Albuquerque long enough to contract smallpox, and he brought the dread disease with him to Savoia . . . ." The smallpox epidemic which resulted quickly spread to Zuni, and by the following year, the missionaries reported that they would not go to the pueblo "for the reason that the smallpox was raging among the Indians."[310]

Nearly a dozen of the Mormon settlers died from smallpox, but they persisted in their attempt to colonize Zuni territory and tried to cure the Zunis through their ministrations. Early in 1878, Llewelyn Harris blessed, through the "laying on of hands," 406 Zunis, all of whom he claimed to have cured. This account has remained rather famous in Mormon journals as an example of miraculous healing. H. K. Palmer, who was now a Presbyterian minister on the reservation became quite jealous and ordered Harris off the premises. Reportedly he spread a rumor that the Zunis "were healed by the power of the devil."[311] It was also reported that the Mormons evacuated Savoia as a result of the disease.

Whether or not the Zunis were healed, the net result of this Mormon/smallpox contact was disaster for them. Between 150 and 200 Zunis had died by February 1878, and the disease continued on through part of 1879, when it was reported that many of the 44 students in the Presbyterian school had passed away.[312] It is likely that the actual death count ran much higher. In 1882 one author said, "It is only a few years since the Zunis numbered several thousand, but an epidemic of the smallpox decimated them horribly."[313]

In 1871 the United States formally ended the policy of treaty making with tribes. At the same time, government effort to control tribal affairs and prevent traditional activities increased. A curtailment of "local political autonomy often came with or shortly after, the commencement of reservation life."[314] This loss of internal political control was about to overcome Pedro Pino and the

Zunis. In 1876 settlers had begun moving into the area around Zuni in much greater numbers: The Zunis had allowed Mormons to settle to the east of them, Navajos were coming closer and closer on the north and east, and Spanish-speaking people were pushing toward the Zunis' southern territory. Lawlessness reigned in much of the area outside of Pino's domain, as evidenced by the request by Indian Agent Thomas in 1876 for an escort of four or five men just so he could visit the pueblo of Zuni.[315] At most of the other pueblos in New Mexico, efforts were being made to survey the grant boundaries.[316] At Zuni a reservation by executive order of Congress was in the works.

Thomas had recognized that four leagues would not be sufficient land for the Zunis. He asked the surveyor of the territorial line, Chandler Robbins, to help him determine the size of a reservation for the tribe. He used the surveyor's description without, apparently, ever consulting Pino or the Zunis to prepare the reservation boundaries, which he then submitted to the president. Later, Thomas would claim that Chandler had "misled" him and that much Zuni land was omitted, but in the meantime, on March 16, 1877, a "large" reservation was set aside for the use of the Zuni Indians.[317]

The reservation would go through a number of changes in the coming years. There was a series of "land-grabbing" attempts and responses by the government, until the reservation today includes a total of something over four hundred thousand acres. This is about 3 percent of the area controlled by the Zunis when Pino took office as governor. For more than 250 years, a half century longer than the present life of the United States, the Zunis had held onto their land even though they were under European domination. Now in 1877, a little more than thirty years after the arrival of the United States in the Southwest, tragedy struck. The Zunis began to lose legal title to, and much of the use of, more than fourteen million acres—with no recompense!

nine
Reservation and Retirement: "I Have Been a Great Captain"

Indian Agent Ben Thomas's request to the commissioner of Indian affairs was submitted on February 28, 1877. It began,

> The Pueblos of Zuni, like the other eighteen Pueblos of this Agency, have a land-grant from the Spanish Government, but unlike those of most of the other Pueblos, the Zuni grant is nearly worthless, and if the Zuni Indians were restricted to their grant, they could not possibly maintain themselves nor their stock, consisting as it does of a sand-bed two leagues [*sic*] square. These Indians have hitherto supported themselves by farming outlying arable lands at or near . . . "Nutrias," "Ojo Pescado," and "Ojo Caliente," and many small patches of land on the course of the stream.[318] . . . The Indians have held and farmed it from time immemorial and have firmly believed, and still believe, that it belongs to them; but now as the country settles up, they are being crowded more and more, year by year, and if some protection is not guaranteed them, they will soon lose their only means of subsistence.[319]

Thomas went on to describe a tract of land intended to include the three main farming villages, then countered potential negative arguments about the size of the reservation:

> It may be objected that this tract is unnecessarily large for fifteen hundred Indians and their stock, but when it is considered that nearly all of it is nearly or quite barren, I hope that it will be conceded that it is none too large. The other Pueblos hold their land

by quit-claim title from the United States, but this plan seems to work evil in that such a title seems to confer the right to sell the land, at least, there is much trouble growing out of this question continually, and it is difficult to prevent individual Indians from squandering the land of different communities. For these reasons it would seem much better in this case simply to withdraw this tract from sale and entry and set it apart as a reservation for the use of the Zuni Indians as long as they occupy it . . . it [the boundary description] is believed to be nearly correct. There are, at present, no settlers within the limits proposed, and I am confident that there is no adverse claim to any portion of the tract.[320]

During the same month, Thomas informed Governor Pino that the tribe no longer could control their salt lake the same way they had since aboriginal times.[321] Pino was beginning to feel the immediate loss of autonomy which came with reservation life. Also during February, Thomas licensed another trader to work at Zuni, the first of three who were approved during 1877.[322]

Then, on June 27, 1877, Pino received the news about the reservation. Thomas blandly announced to old Pedro Pino that a reservation had been set aside for the Zuni people and that he was busy finding another teacher for the pueblo. "I send you today," Thomas reported, "an order from the President giving you a large Reservation for the use of the Pueblo of Zuni." And then with hardly a breath between, Thomas went on about the teacher, "I am trying to find a good teacher with a family, to go to Zuni to live with you for the purpose of teaching all the children of the Pueblo and helping you to keep away people from this land which the President has given you."[323]

Thomas negotiated with the Presbyterian Board of Home Missions and finally contracted with H. K. Palmer to act as teacher at Zuni for six hundred dollars a year.[324] The old governor was deluged with new restrictions and obligations as a result. A fair example of the government's new attitude toward Pino's authority was illustrated in the agent's instructions to the Zuni governor regarding the new reservation school. Pino was ordered to find a house for the teacher and a home for the school; he was told to require the people to send their children to school and sell food to the teacher ("you have fat sheep to sell"), supply the school with firewood, and fill the quota of four hundred children in the school every day.[321]

It must have reminded old Governor Pino of the Spanish mission system, from which he had escaped as a youth. And these were not the only problems Pedro Pino faced on the new reservation. The smallpox epidemic of 1878 was raging so badly that the new teacher temporarily left Zuni by February, and the troops at Fort Wingate were being inoculated.[322] Another problem came from Santiago Baca, one of the two new traders licensed at Zuni in 1878. Baca almost immediately got into trouble with the Zunis when he settled on property which had been improved by the people but was outside the new limits of the reservation, near Ojo Caliente. Pino complained to the agent that Baca was on Zuni land, but Thomas responded that the trader was within his rights and the Zunis had better not molest him.[327] Pedro Pino was quickly learning what a reservation meant and how much land the Zunis had lost. It must have been a crushing experience for the man who had spent his entire life fighting to preserve those ancient Zuni boundaries.

Life at Zuni was apparently too hard on Dr. Palmer, the teacher, and in the spring he closed the school and left the pueblo for good. Thomas reported that it was a result of Palmer's failed health and promised a new teacher in the near future—a promise that may have sounded more like a threat to Governor Pino. Until this time, the Zunis had supplied housing for the teacher at no cost. Thomas reported that the next teacher would be authorized to build a school.[328] Pino must have wondered where that authorization would come from and who was going to pay for the land the school would be built on. It was becoming evident that the Zunis were no longer the autonomous tribe they had been for so many years. Pino's authority was eroding daily.

But Pino was not completely forgotten. Authorities knew that he was the expert on that area of New Mexico and Arizona, and so when dignitaries visited, they stopped to talk with him. In 1878 one of the most important military leaders in the United States army made a visit to the Southwest to survey the country which the railroad would soon be forging across. General William Tecumseh Sherman had said, before a House Committee, that he thought both Arizona and New Mexico should be given back to old Mexico. After his visit, he changed his mind and agreed that the area had potential.[329]

During the course of his trip, Sherman determined to visit Governor Pino, perhaps having read one of the recent articles written by Francis Klett or reviewed Wheeler's reports. At any rate, Pueblo Agent Thomas wrote to Governor Pino. "I have to inform you," Thomas began, "that General Sherman is now here enroute from Washington to Zuni to make the people of Zuni a visit. I cannot tell you just when he will arrive at your Pueblo, but he will probably get there in about fifteen days from the present time. General Sherman," Thomas emphasized, "is one of the greatest men in the United States and he is the first in command of the United States Army. He commands all the soldiers."

One must wonder if Pino recognized a new patronizing tone in the letters now coming from the U.S. Indian agent, if he noted how the agent belabored every point as though all that the old governor had done for the past thirty years had been for naught. "Now I want the people of Zuni to treat the General with great respect," Thomas continued. "He has talked with me about you and is very desirous of seeing you at home. I know it is only necessary for me to make the request of you in order to secure to the General the kind treatment which I desire for him. "[330]

The only record we have of the meeting between Sherman and Pino is the note the general left with the governor. Sherman reported that Pino had shown him his letters of testimonial, including an 1848 document, which must have been the agreement with the United States that he had signed. Sherman said he personally knew most of the men who had written these testimonials and that the documents entitled "him personally [Pino] and his people to the friendly conduct of all Americans. I commend him to all who pass this way, and recommend that the farms, gardens, stock, and property of the Zunis be respected. They seem industrious, friendly and worthy, because they are self maintaining." Then in a parting comment Sherman praised Pino once more: "Pedro Pino seems to be the Ancient of the village and knows all its past history and the road which leads to every point of the compass."[331]

Pedro Pino did indeed know all of the pueblo's past history, and it must have been lying very heavily on his mind. The year 1878 was Pedro Pino's last as governor of Zuni. After a brief interruption of his duties, evidently necessitated by his age, he was again offered the position of governor by the *caciques*. Old Pino was nearing ninety and declined the offer; instead, he nominated his son Ba:lawahdiwa (Patricio Pino) as his successor.[332]

The story of Ba:lawahdiwa is as long and interesting as his father's, but it is another story, one about the governor of Zuni fighting to keep the reservation, an orator who talked to audiences throughout the nation, a man caught in the middle of intense political maneuvering as different power groups tried to gain control of the Zuni people. With the establishment of the reservation, a new chapter began for the Zuni people. Pedro Pino had led them well up to this point, but it must have been a great tragedy for him to see so much of his land lost and the authority of the position of governor usurped.

Old Pedro Pino continued to advise the *caciques* and help his son in difficult situations, but he turned most of his attention to his gardens and fields. Five or six years later, Cushing commented that since his resignation, "he has . . . been constantly occupied with his agricultural pursuits, as well as with his duties as ecclesiastical chief of his clan, and Keeper of the Amulets of the Hunt."[333]

But it was not long before Pedro Pino was back in the thick of a political controversy. In early 1879, Patricio Pino was arrested and jailed for assault. Pedro Pino sought help through the agent. Unable to write himself, he asked the wife of the new schoolteacher to write to Thomas for him. While Pino had been following his retirement pursuits, a new schoolteacher, T. F. Ealy, had arrived at Zuni in 1878 with his wife and rented a house from old Pedro. Almost immediately Ealy had tried to come to the aid of the Zunis by keeping the agent informed of Navajo depredations and, apparently, arranging for a shipment of plows to the pueblo.[334]

The new Zuni governor was deluged with problems during his first days in office. Ealy immediately tried to oust any Mormons from the reservation, and a controversy started over the number of missionaries who should be on the reservation. Navajos were herding their flocks of sheep into the grain fields near the farming villages. Mexican Americans were settling in traditional Zuni areas. The school was opening full-time. The agent asked for a wagon load of pottery, apparently for a government sponsored study. And finally, to add insult to a delicate situation, Thomas invited Patricio to Santa Fe to instruct him on how to run the pueblo.[335]

Patricio declined the invitation to visit Santa Fe and did not send any pottery to the agent (in the coming years, many individuals and expeditions would buy, trade, and steal much of the material wealth of Zuni—pottery, jewelry and religious artifacts). The trespassing of Navajos and Mexican Americans was not so easily avoided. Patricio was involved in meetings and councils and ordered trespassers to leave, but apparently he was finally forced to remove one man himself. As a result, Patricio and two other Zunis were arrested and jailed in Los Lunas.

Pedro asked Mrs. Ealy to write Thomas and explain that the Mexican was trespassing and there was no assault. The case finally went to trial, and Governor Patricio Pino was acquitted. However, his horses were confiscated for court costs! This was Patricio's early initiation into the American justice system.[336] Pedro must have taken cold comfort from the fact that his son had to deal with the problems now.

The floodgates were now open. Patricio had to deal with extortion attempts, robbers, trespassers, surveying parties, squatters, and any number of other problems caused by the influx of whites into the area. But newcomers were still met with the same hospitality shown at the pueblo for centuries. In October 1879, a surveying party for the railroad reached the vicinity of Zuni, causing much excitement at the pueblo. Eventually the railroad would follow the valley of the Rio Puerco, but these surveyors were mapping a route closer to the pueblo. When they arrived at Zuni, Governor Patricio Pino appointed three men to accompany the party as guides "and point out the best route through their country."[337] The guides were reportedly successful: "The route they designated proved to be excellent, nearly devoid of hills, with frequent springs of water, and with grass in abundance. It is probably not too much to say that there is no people on the continent, enlightened or otherwise, among whom the laws are executed with greater regularity and efficiency than they are among these Pueblos."[338]

It was against this backdrop that anthropologists, or ethnologists, as they were commonly called then, arrived at Zuni. Late in September of 1879, a government party led by Colonel James Stevenson came to Zuni. The party and its members were highly important to the Zunis for many years to come. Under Major John Wesley Powell, the Bureau of American Ethnology (BAE) had commissioned parties to go among some of the Indian tribes and collect art and artifacts. Powell was afraid that the material and social cultures of the Indians would soon disappear if they were not quickly recorded.

Stevenson's expedition was the first of several to go to the Zuni Pueblo and acquire, in one way or another, thousands of pots, blankets, and other objects. An employee of the BAE, who was on this first expedition and had shown remarkable ethnological ability at a young age, had also been commissioned by Powell to stay at the pueblo for several months and study the Zunis' religion and culture. This young man was Frank Hamilton Cushing. His presence would have a tremendous impact on the future of the pueblo and its political relations with the government for many years.

As the expedition departed from Zuni, Cushing stayed behind, as though abandoned, and the Zunis, true to custom, took pity on him, fed him, clothed him, and finally adopted him and allowed him to join several of their secret and sacred societies. He stayed at Zuni longer than his commission—four and a half years—all the while writing about the religious ceremonies of the tribe. He used his influence to pressure the tribe into following his advice, at times even resorted to military might to gain what he wanted, but on the whole was a friend of the Zunis and seems to have been truly converted to the Ashiwi. His work is a marvelous account of Zuni life, but there were consequences which he could not have seen at the time.

Cushing, called by some the father of anthropology and by others "the first professional field ethnologist," is recognized today as "the earliest professional anthropologist to so completely identify with and integrate into Indian society."[339] He eventually signed his letters as "1st War Chief of Zuni and Asst. U.S. Ethnologist," an intriguing fusion of two different cultures. He was quickly adopted by Patricio Pino as a brother (a man without a family in Zuni was in trouble). Thus, Cushing came to know not only Patricio but his father, Pedro Pino, as well. Through all that went on during the nearly five years he was at Zuni, the relationship between Cushing and the Pinos grew and flourished. Cushing did his level best to protect the tribe from a number of threats which he saw to their existence—land-grab attempts, Navajo rustling, white outlaws, and corrupt politicians and Indian agents. Many whites visited the pueblo to see the people Cushing wrote about in his nationally syndicated articles—and kept quite secret from the tribe. Newspapermen, writers, and other ethnologists came in ever-increasing numbers.[340]

Now more than ninety years old, Pedro Pino paid most of his attention to his religious duties and tending his gardens and fields. But the elder statesman was not yet free from Zuni business. In 1880 Pino was called to Santa Fe to file a deposition with the surveyor general concerning the Zunis' land grant.[341] Ethnologist Matilda Coxe Stevenson complimented Pedro Pino in 1881: "Though holding no official position his fluency in speaking Spanish, together with his mature judgement and good sense, commands for him a high seat in the councils of his people." His enduring friendship for the Americans was illustrated in her following comment: "Appreciating the advantages of education, he is anxious to have the youth of the pueblo taught English."[342]

Old Pedro's friendship for the whites did not make him immune to badgering from some of them, even in his later years. In May of 1881, another ethnologist, John C. Bourke, who was also an army officer, visited Zuni to meet the people and make a report to General Sheridan on their condition. Bourke was accompanied by the prominent artist, Willard L. Metcalf, and Sylvester Baxter, a reporter for the *Boston Herald* and *Harper's.*[343]

When Bourke reached the pueblo, he found that Cushing was violently ill, and so, because the army officers at Fort Wingate had told him that Pedro Pino knew more than anyone else about the Zunis' customs and history, he searched him out and questioned the former Zuni governor.[344]

"I see you have on a uniform," the old governor said when Bourke entered his room. "Wait a moment until I put on my good clothing." The old man produced a red flannel, long-tailed shirt, which he donned before resuming the conversation in his perfect Spanish.

Bourke faithfully recorded in his journals the conversations which took place. Some of this dialogue is a fine example of the way early ethnologists and later anthropologists extracted information from Indians. Bourke immediately began to quiz the old man, pausing only for a few preliminary flatteries.

"It was asserted by some ignorant people that the Zunis were not a bit different from the wild Indians who roamed the plains and were only a little above the level of the brute, but *I* knew better than this," Bourke said, "and wished that Pedro would give me a list of the families or clans of his people so that I could show the white men when I returned to Washington that the Zunis were a most excellent race, equal to the Americans in every respect."[345]

Admitting that he resorted to "flattery" and "exaggeration," Bourke reported that Pino initially gave the officer/scientist some valuable information. In response to questions about the project engrossing him when Bourke arrived, Pino explained, "These feathers, you see, are to bring us rain. All the Zunis will plant these feather sticks in the ground and water will come down on their crops." Pino, who had been married for a great many years, explained his kin and clan in a few brief words: "I, Pedro Pino, am one of the Aquila (eagle) clan, but my wife belongs to the Guacamayo (Parrot) clan, and all my children belong to the same clan. And I live with my wife's people but when *I* die the Eagle clan will bury *me,* because I am Eagle and have been a great captain in that clan."[346]

Pino was also willing to give Bourke a list of the clans at Zuni at that time.[347] He explained that his grandson Napoleon was the governor of Acoma, but Pino refused to give any information about some things. He was willing to explain the political structure of the tribe and describe some of the customs and games, but when asked to provide the Indian names of some of the men, he refused. And when Bourke asked Pedro Pino if he could accompany him to plant the prayer feathers he had been assembling, Pino had to draw the line.

"My friend," responded Pino, "everybody in this world has his own business to attend to; for instance, there is the maestro (i.e., the school-master, the missionary, Reverend Dr. Ealy), he has his business, he teaches school; then there is Mr. Graham, he has his business, he sells flour and sugar and coffee in his store, and I have my business, *I* am going to plant these feathers and so, everybody has his own business."[348]

With the influx of missionaries, anthropologists, government agents, military personnel, and settlers into the Zuni area, it became more and more difficult to determine who, in fact, was the true spokesman for the U.S. government. Cushing, to gain the Zunis'confidence to further his studies and gather ethnological information, competed with the missionaries, the teacher, and sometimes the agent for authority at the pueblo. The new school-teacher was especially resentful of Cushing's presence and attitude. As an ethnologist and member of the Priesthood of the Bow, Cushing seemed to support the native religion, while the new teacher/missionary opposed the "pagan" beliefs of the people.

The Reverend Samuel A. Bentley replaced Ealy as teacher in 1881. Ealy was still renting his living quarters from Pedro Pino because all building materials were being diverted for railroad construction. Before he left, he complained that Cushing was interfering with the operation of the school, and the controversy continued when Bentley arrived and took up the argument. Another person who opposed Cushing was Matilda Coxe Stevenson, wife of Colonel James Stevenson and herself a fledgling ethnologist. Cushing and Stevenson did not get along from the first, and Bourke complained that she "monopolized all the available eggs and milk at the pueblo."[349]

Bentley and Stevenson apparently went to Pedro Pino and suggested that Cushing was a fraud, "a nobody, and of no importance."[350] Pino then went to Bourke and asked him for the truth. Bourke impressed the retired governor with the fact that he was an army official and then produced an official-looking Smithsonian report, saying that Cushing had contributed to it and Bentley was a liar. As for Stevenson, Bourke commented that "she didn't know anything about it."[351] Pino believed Bourke's statements and impressed by his uniform, and he accompanied Bourke throughout the rest of his stay at the pueblo as interpreter and guide.

Privately Cushing told Bourke that he was afraid the Zunis would discover his trickery (publishing their esoteric knowledge), and he would be forced to flee the pueblo. Cushing had refused, thus far, to take a Zuni wife, and so the Zunis, in turn, were beginning to suspect that he was merely trying to learn their secrets. Pedro Pino went to Bourke with this accusation and explained that with he had learned, Cushing would not be allowed to leave the pueblo.

"But then he can never take my old friend, Pedro Pino, to Washington, to see the Great Father, to take him by the hand, see the wonderful sights of the Estados Unidos, and receive beautiful presents from the Americans," Bourke replied.[352]

Cushing confided to Bourke that

> as he continued to refuse to take a Zuni wife, he feared that the Zuni would become convinced that he had duped them in order to learn their secrets. For the present he felt fairly safe, holding out to them the promised trip to Washington as reward for being admitted further into their esoteric life. Within six months or so he expected he would have penetrated to the "Arcana of Zuni traditions" and after that he would have to be ready for flight.[353]

Another problem which faced Cushing was the growing number of Mormon converts. Non-Mormon officials at the pueblo claimed that the Mormons opposed the federal government in their policy with the Zunis (as well as other tribes) and were encouraging the Zunis to ally themselves with Salt Lake City and not Washington. In a show of force, Cushing and Bourke sent troops to arrest a leading Mormon Zuni named Ramon Luna.[354] Luna was forced to pledge his allegiance to the United States and deny the authority of the Mormon church. Through this demonstration, Cushing convinced the Zuni leaders that the government was indeed backing him and thus was able to prolong his stay at the pueblo without having to marry a member of the tribe. Pedro Pino also talked to Bourke about the Mormon situation. He reported that he had been baptized but it had been accomplished by trickery. Pino told Bourke that he felt "chagrin, for he was a Washington man, not a Mormon, and he wanted Bourke to make this clear in Washington."[355]

Cushing vehemently denied the accusation by Bentley that he was deceiving the people, though it was at least partly true. Cushing wrote to his superiors in Washington, describing Bentley's charges. "He has constantly been casting mud and slime in my pathway, by telling the Indians I was not what I had been representing myself, that I had come here to write about all their secret affairs, and when I sent my papers East, I was paid for them and that was the way I was enabled to live."[356] Eventually, when Pino was caught in the middle of the deception, Cushing was forced to call him a "liar" to avoid admitting that he was one.

Cushing also showed Bentley his bracelet of small sea shells and pointed out that it meant he was a member of the Priesthood of the Bow: "Each member of our order was sworn to eternal fraternity and fidelity, and that *once* a Priest of the Bow *always* so. . . ."[357] Cushing's sense of "fraternity" and "fidelity" was quite malleable according to the ends he wished to accomplish. His work, as noted earlier, is marvelous in its authenticity and detail, but the effects of his deceptions and manipulating at the pueblo lingered long after. Pedro Pino found himself caught in "a center of controversy in the village over acceptance of new ways, a controversy which during the 1880s developed into mild factionalism."[358]

In fact, the divisive politics fostered in the pueblo by Cushing, Bentley, Bourke, and others were partly responsible for serious factionalism and division for decades to come. Historian Oakah L. Jones commented on Cushing's behavior at the pueblo. "He certainly antagonized the Zunis repeatedly in his early activities—a defiance which today simply would not be tolerated in any pueblo of New Mexico. In the end, he violated Zunis' trust by publishing many of the secret legends and ceremonial practices of his adopted nation."[359] Zuni tradition today suggests that after Cushing's adoption, disasters began to befall the tribe, a correct historical observation whatever the cause may be.

Bourke continued to encourage Pino's beliefs about the power of Washington. In 1880 and 1881, the railroad was finally coming into Zuni country. During both of these years, all the able and willing men from the pueblos of Zuni, Acoma, and Laguna were working to lay the tracks.[360] Bourke told Pino that "the Rail Road at Wingate [A&P] would soon give the Zuni a fine market for all their manufactures and products—silverware, blankets, pottery, eggs, chickens, corn, fruits, and vegetables."[361]

Nothing could have been further from the truth. The railroad brought homesteaders to settle on former Zuni land. It brought produce from the outside, destroying what trade the Zunis had left with the military. Army officers began grazing their own stock and forming cattle companies (like Washington Matthews at Fort Wingate, whose company *owned no land at all*). The railroad intensified the loss of Zuni aboriginal holdings. The military and the B.A.E. sent joint expeditions to gather more Zuni artifacts for the Smithsonian Institution. Thousands of pots, many, many wagon loads, were taken to Washington, where they still fill corridors of storage space in the Smithsonian. Records do not indicate adequate payment to the Zunis.

Bourke summed up his propagandistic speech:

> And a little farther on, the Rail Road would approach a lot tumble-down rookeries on top of rocky mesas, and the Americans on the cars would ask "who are those naked, half-starved old men up there? Why! don't you know? Those are the Moquis [Hopi], the friends of the Mormons." The Mormons came to them and wanted to be their friends and asked for a little land. The Moquis gave it. By and by the Mormons grew strong and first took away the cottonfields of the Oraybes at Mayencope (laughter among the Zunis). And afterwards the peach orchards and fields of the villages themselves. Then they took away all the women, because every Mormon wants 7 or 8 women and the Moquis had to go without; and all the good the Mormons ever did the Moquis was go baptize them in a cold spring two or three times a week and give them a bad attack of rheumatism or make their teeth ache and their throat choke just as Pedro Pino's did when they baptized him.[362]

All of the pressure from Cushing and Bourke strengthened Pedro Pino's belief in the power of Washington and his policy of friendship toward the great nation. Cushing's description of Pino as "Cazique Grande"[363] was likely correct in political matters. Even though he was retired, his opinions must have carried a good deal of weight. Bourke reinforced Pino's support for the government by paying fifteen dollars for the old man's services as guide and interpreter when he finally left the village.[364] Pino supported Cushing, but he still believed that the ethnologist should marry a Zuni and raise a family, like any respectable man. It was becoming clear to Cushing that he would actually have to take some of the Zunis to Washington to continue his work at Zuni.

ten
Though Your Body Perish

In 1882 Frank Cushing arranged the long-awaited trip to the East Coast for Pedro Pino and several other Zunis. He arranged the trip so that he might obtain more funding for his research at Zuni, impress the Zunis with American might, and allow himself to be initiated into some secret Zuni orders which he had been unable to enter.[365] Cushing also managed to find an American wife, thus avoiding any further problems with marriage at the pueblo.

Pedro Pino had long been promised (by various government officials) the chance to visit the great American cities and see the actual ruling body of the country. This hardy old man was not completely through with his career. Before he passed on, he participated in one further adventure, one which to him was perhaps the greatest adventure of all. Though ninety and some years of age, he consented to go. Cushing reported,

> When reminded of his great age and infirmities, of the immense distance to be traveled over, and of the possible consequence of change in food and climate, he remarked: "I have but a few days, as it were, to live. If disappointed, I must die ere the return of the pilgrims. If permitted to join your party, through the happiness of my heart and the joy of meeting my brothers of old Washington times, it may be I shall grow young again. Or, if I should die! What Matters it? At best, I have but a few days to live."[366]

Thus, in February of 1882, Pino, aged and wrinkled, and about one hundred years old, joined the party to the East Coast. Cushing described the rest of the group:

Nai iu tchi, First Cacique of War, Master of the Esoteric Priesthood of the Bow and Warrior of the Order of the Cactus, or Surgeon.

Ki a si, Second Cacique of War, Second Master of the Priesthood of the Bow and Warrior of the order of the Wolf, or Hunters.

Lai iu aih tsai lun kia, Second Cacique of Peace, and Master Medicine man of the order of Fire. (My [Cushing's] father by personal and clan adoption.)

Pa lo wah ti wa [Patricio Pino or Ba:lawahdiwa], Governor or Head secular Chief of the Zunis, and Warrior of the order of Fire. (My brother by clan and war adoption.)[367]

One other participant in the journey to Washington, D.C., was Nanahe, described by Cushing as a Hopi "who had been adopted into the nation by marriage, a youthful-looking man of thirty-five years, and a member of the Order of the Lesser Fire."[368] Cushing described Pedro Pino as "former Head Chief of the Zunis for more than thirty years (Father of the present Hd. Chief) and warrior of the order of Great Coals."[369] Newspaperman Sylvester Baxter's account of the journey denoted Pedro Pino as "governor of Zuni for thirty years, now a wrinkled old man of between eighty and ninety years."[370]

Near Fort Wingate, where the railroad had recently been completed, Pedro saw a locomotive for the first time. Though it must have seemed a monstrous sight, he never flinched but performed the prayers and ceremonies which his religion dictated. The party then boarded the train and departed for the "ocean of sunrise." The people had packed large quantities of Zuni food, fearing that the American food might disagree with them. Sure enough, when one Zuni tried too much of the rich, foreign cuisine, he commented, "My inside is not only filled with food but also with much fighting." The Zunis' assessment was that "they thought the Americans ate too many things and dared their insides."[371]

Food aside, Cushing was gaining his desired effect: The Zunis were suitably impressed. On the second day of their journey, at the engineer's request, Cushing brought Nai-iu-tchi to the engine. According to Baxter, the chief priest of the bow, "who was always ready for anything, stood unmoved while the whistle was blown at its shrillest, and regarding reverently the action of the locomotive, he exclaimed: 'The Americans are gods, only they have to eat material food.'"372 The group made headlines as it crossed the country. Newspapers commented on every step of the journey, with one article mentioning another of Cushing's motives: "He hopes to get an increase in their allotment of territory as their herds and flocks have not sufficient grazing range."373

The group first stopped at Chicago, where the Zunis marveled at the architecture and commented that their hotel was a pueblo in itself. Then it was on to Washington. Pedro Pino, long the ally of the Americans and political leader of the pueblo, felt that he had reached the pinnacle of his career. The crowning moment of his life came when he met President Chester A. Arthur and was able to grasp his hand and breathe a prayer onto it. He was moved to tears.

His emotion was greater, though, when he visited Washington's tomb at Mount Vernon. There, said Cushing, Pedro Pino wept uncontrollably: "He regarded Washington as the Great Cacique of the American chiefs he had known during the prime of his life, and mourned that he should never have had an opportunity of grasping him by the hand."374 Then he climbed to the top of the Washington Monument against Cushing's strenuous advice. Cushing said that Pino was "too feeble and must not climb to the top of that 'Standing White Rock' of Was´-sin'tona." But Pino waited until Cushing was gone and, claiming that he was "a mere youngster, anyway, and had no business to forbid his praying to the Sun Father whencesoever he pleased," sneaked out and made his trek. Some time later Washington police brought the old Zuni leader home. His companions reported that "a little while ago some Me-li-kana-kwe in blue breeches and yellow buttons [policemen] brought him home and said much, but we could not understand them."

Evidently the climb was a severe ordeal because, when Cushing arrived on the scene, "the old man was stretched out on the floor groaning piteously and writhing under the bony hands of Lai ia-ah-tsai-lun-k'ia, the medicine-man of the party. The others were sitting around looking dark and out of sorts." In fact, one of the others, fearing that Pino had brought shame to the

Zuni nation, commented, "May the old burro be reduced to the eating of cedar-bark!"[375]

Pedro's son, the present Governor Patricio, had a somewhat different perspective on the "Standing White Rock." He climbed to the top of the monument, looked out at the scene before him, and commented, "No longer the powerful Americans, but little men like ants creeping around on the ground below, and horses no larger than mice, and instead of the great Potomac, a little stream hardly larger than the Zuni River."[376] Patricio was impressed with a comic opera he attended, *The Mascotte*, which provided him with tunes he sang at Zuni for months after. But, he said, the great numbers of people in Chicago caused him bewilderment and wonder.[377]

Nai-iu-tchi, the chief priest of the bow, sounded more like a tourist when he later recalled Jumbo the elephant and said he was the most wonderful animal he had ever seen, and bigger than he supposed the gods created them. Then he added, gleefully, "I have his picture in my little treasure box."

When asked what pleased him most of all he saw on the trip, Nai-iu-tchi supposedly responded, "The sea lions at Lincoln Park!" This was, according to one account, because "they were the first creatures carrying life in their breasts he had ever seen that came from the ocean, which the Zunis worship. Like other people they worship that which they deem most precious. With the Zunis it is the water of the sea, the river and the spring; that which alone stands between them and starvation in this parched and arid land."[378] When asked which of the white man's ways was most impressive, Nai-iu-tchi replied, "The ease with which they can get water. The white man takes the river into the walls of his house. By turning a little iron stick he can get that which we pray for all our lives."[379]

Unfortunately, Pedro Pino missed seeing the sea lions, the "ocean of sunrise," and the "sleight of hand men" or jugglers in New York who so impressed the others in the group. The elder Pino grew sick from all the exertion and had to stay with Colonel and Mrs. Stevenson in Washington while the rest of the party went on to Boston and the Atlantic seacoast, where ceremonies were performed by the ocean. But he recovered after only a few days in

Washington and quickly took to the customs of the Americans, even deigning to use a finger bowl and adapting to silverware. Undoubtedly Stevenson's wife, Matilda (Tillie) Coxe, was already becoming enamored with the ways of the Zunis from her talks with wise old Pedro. After her husband died, she eventually moved to Zuni and wrote one of the more thorough ethnological studies on the Indians (although the Zunis find many inaccuracies today).

The elder Pino continued to make the acquaintance of many notables around Washington. After meeting the president of the United States, he spoke with the speaker of the House of Representatives, the Honorable John G. Carlisle. Later, after returning to the pueblo, Pino received a package of garden seeds from Carlisle, with a note attached, "Hoping that you may live many years yet to counsel and help your people."[380] Years later, when near death, We wha, a prominent Zuni, remembered the gift and called the congressman "Captain Carlisle, the great seed priest."[381]

Through the years that he had dealt with the Americans, Pino had noticed that these people kept photos of their dead and paintings of their admired leaders and famous citizens. Earlier in the year at the pueblo, when he had watched the artist Metcalf paint a portrait of his son, Pedro had said to Patricio, "Though your body perish, nevertheless you shall continue to live on upon the earth. Your face will not be forgotten now; though your hair turn gray, it will never turn gray here, I know this to be so for I have seen, in the quarters of the officers at the fort, the faces of their fathers, who have long since passed from the earth, but still were looking down upon their children from the walls."[382] While in Washington, old Pedro Pino had another memorable moment. He sat for photographic portraits before the camera of John C. Hillers, Powell's well-known photographer, the first person to photograph the Grand Canyon.

The visit to Washington was not without its humorous moments. Pino and the other Zunis believed that they would insult their hosts if they did not eat each meal, and even each course offered to them, including a liberal amount of the condiments on the table. During one meal, aboard a train out of Chicago, a member of the Zuni party complained about the American food's spiciness.

"Would you have me cover my nation with shame?" retorted Pedro Pino, as he accepted a lemon which a generous passenger had just given him, meaning that he was obliged to try either everything offered to him or nothing and maintain himself on his Zuni corn food.

"What though we be wafted in this swift wagon as on the wings of the wind!" he continued, pulling out his hunting knife and flourishing the lemon. "Is it not a house with many sitters?" he commented on the train as he examined the fruit. "It must be some kind of little melon," he finally decided and severed the lemon.

> Pino, of course, had never tasted anything like a lemon, nor even a spoonful of acid, save such a mild suggestion of it as might have lodged in a green peach or resulted from the fermentation of meat stew. . . . he buried his toothless gums in the major half of it—but the next instant the lemon was rolling on the floor, and he off his seat! He seized his chops with both hands; tears oozed from his close-shut eyes; he wriggled, groaned, hawked, bent far over the aisle, retched, heaved—and one of his companions remarked, "Well he has covered his nation with shame after all!" But the old man did not hear.[383]

Though sick and worn out from the journey east, Pino returned to Zuni without complaint and within a short time had recovered his health. The trip had made a strong impression on the old man. He had been taken by everything the Americans represented (the only thing the Zunis said the Americans were second best at was painting: The Japanese excelled them). Pino continued to use his influence at the pueblo. It is unfortunate that the last mentions of him show that he was, after his return from Washington, placed in the midst of a flowering controversy among the people of the pueblo.

General John A. Logan,[384] soon to be a candidate in the presidential election of 1884, visited Nutria, one of the springs of the Zunis. He and a group of his relatives determined that the spring, town of Nutria, and farmland were not strictly inside the reservation boundaries, though the description had clearly intended them to be. They filed claims on the land.[385] Thus, the powerful Americans whom Pino had befriended were now attempting to steal what land the Zunis had left, and this particular area was some of the more important acreage the Zunis still owned. Even worse, from Pino's view, than the actions of Logan's relatives were those of the President. President Arthur vacillated with the pressures of election-year politics, and, even though the Zunis had met him and breathed prayers on his hand, he did not support them. After the election, in one of his last acts in office, Arthur signed an executive order which apparently allowed the Logan group to keep the Zunis' land.[386] Cushing and his friends in the East eventually managed to save the land for the Zunis, but not before Logan forced Cushing out of the pueblo[387] (he would return with the Hemenway Southwestern Archeological Expedition a few years later).

The involvement of the Zunis in national politics did not help their tribal affairs at home. Pino was now, in his last years, in the center of developing factionalism at the pueblo His old "friend," Colonel Stevenson, reportedly said of the Zunis at this time, "They are wretchedly ignorant and degraded by the crudest superstition. They are today the most religious people on the continent."[388] The latter statement is a strange insult, but no stranger than the statements in the New Mexico papers, which attacked Cushing for siding with the Indians, saying he was "the greatest fraud and biggest ass that ever crossed her [New Mexico's] borders." When his ineptitude was brought to the attention of the Bureau of Indian Affairs, one article surmised that Cushing would have to "take off his 'gee-string' [and] once more don the habiliment of civilization."[389] In the heat of the national election, it was charged that the Zunis were "worthless lazy vagabonds" and had never used Nutria Springs.[390] Even more absurd was the suggestion that, if the Zunis had had any ambition, they would have filed a claim on the springs themselves.[391]

So Pedro Pino's last days were evidently filled with this terrible controversy in the pueblo. The very friends he had cultivated in Washington seem to have turned against him and his people. Shortly after, his son was replaced as governor, and voices in council urged violence against the Americans. Although this violence never materialized, the controversy which began during Pino's tenure continued for many years.

A perusal of Pedro Pino's papers reads like a history of the Southwest—Ives, Whipple, Beale, Wheeler, Cushing, Sherman, Bourke, Washington, Pfieffer, and many others. Cushing obtained those papers and included them as part of his own personal collection of manuscripts. Later Frederick Webb Hodge made them part of the archives of the Southwest Museum, where they remain today.

Pino survived capture and imprisonment by the Navajos, servitude among the Mexicans, another near-servitude in the Catholic mission school at Zuni, decades of war with the Navajos and Apaches, the Mexican War, and the War of Rebellion. He saw three corrupt conquering governments and parleyed with each, meeting the foremost leaders of each country and representing his people well. But during the last of his life, he watched his people's land be reduced from millions of acres to a few square miles. Frank Hamilton Cushing lectured throughout the eastern United States for the next ten years and longer about the "fraud and aggressions" of the United States and reported that

> with a sneer of impatience, a gesture of injured deprecation of the narrowness of his present possession, any middle-aged Zuni will define minutely its [the province of the Zunis] boundaries. These were, to the eastward, the plains at the foot of the Gallo Mountains above Agua Fria [Cushing evidently considered the Zuni Mountains as part of a larger range] ; to the northward the Trans-Sierra Valley of the Rio Puerco, from the Longitude of Mount Taylor to the Colorado Chiquito; on the west, in Arizona the latter river nearly to its sources; on the south, after the conquest of Marata, the valleys of the Salt Lake and Rito Quemado, which lie along the bases of the Sierra Datila and Sierra Ladrone. Thus the Cibolan dominion had, from west to east, an extent of one hundred and fifty miles; from north to south, of seventy-five or eighty.[392]

Though Pino watched this great tragedy befall his people, he always met newcomers with hospitality and friendship. The goodwill of his people was often rewarded by American hatred, envy, and jealousy, if not outright theft. He saw his people die of violence, starvation, and foreign disease. And threats from the Americans only increased in future years, when there were attacks, even more serious in nature, on the very beliefs of the Zunis, their religion, and culture.

It is hard to imagine that the strong-willed old man's "heart wore out," but reports and photographs indicate that in old age, he did have "snow upon his head, moss upon his face, bony knees, no longer upright but bent over canes."[393] To the end, whenever Pino's path intersected with another's, he made the commitment: "Sit down. Now speak. I think there is something to say. It will not be too long a talk."[394] One must assume that his "road came in safely," that he traveled on to dwell with the gods beneath the waters of Kolhuwala:wa.

Exactly when old Pedro Pino died is unknown, but he was surely buried by his clan, the Eagle Clan, in the traditional manner of the tribe. Shortly after death, the body was anointed and buried in the sacred graveyard. Cushing described such a burial, saying it ended as the people hastily lowered the body "into a shallow grave, while one standing to the east said a prayer, scattered meal, food, and other offerings upon it; then they as hastily covered it over, clearing away all traces of the new-made grave."[395]

Reflecting on Zunis' death and burial beliefs, Frank Hamilton Cushing summed up their outlook: "A man is like a grain of corn—bury him and he molds; yet his heart lives, and springs out on the breath of life (the soul) to make him as he was, so again."[396]

Afterword

I began my work at Zuni in the late 1960s and early 1970s, help-ing write and publish some curricular materials for the pueblo's schools. Between 1973 and 1974, I worked for Zuni doing a preliminary inquiry into the tribe's potential claim against the United States for lands taken without adequate compensation. An additional section of my report focused on the Zuni Salt Lake and its cultural and historic importance. In 1978, four years after submitting my report to the tribe, Congress passed an act provid-ing jurisdiction for the Zunis to sue the United States. About that time, I began my biography of Lai-iu-ah-tsai-lu, motivated by Cushing's manuscript biography, which I had found at the Southwest Museum, and from reading works like *The Patriot Chiefs* by Alvin Josephy, Jr. I finished the manuscript in 1979 and read a short version of the story that year at Simon Fraser University in Vancouver.[397] I believe I originally intended the larger work for a young Zuni audience. Although my annotations eventually made it a more scholarly work, I have been pleased over the years that the manuscript is popular with Zuni students in the high school.

When I finished the manuscript in 1979, I was director of the Institute of the American West and working on a project and book on the Future of Agriculture in the Rocky Mountains (FARM). That probably explains some of my interest in this book in family farms and ranches in the West. At the same time, I was completing expert testimony for the Zuni court cases. Work on the two claims cases occupied a good deal of my time during the 1980s. When Congress acted to allow the cases, it also authorized the return of the Zuni Salt Lake to the tribe, which occurred during the 1980s.

My part of the work on *A Zuni Atlas,* coauthored by T.J. Ferguson, was completed during my NEH fellowship in 1982 and published by the University of Oklahoma Press in 1985. That work, as well as my book *Zuni and the Courts: A Struggle for Sovereign Land Rights,* published in 1995 by the University Press of Kansas, documents the complicated history and anthropology that was presented to the United States Court of Claims.

The two claims cases were settled in 1990 and resulted in a substantial payment by the United States to the Zuni tribe. During hearings on a congressional bill that eventually settled one of the cases, Floyd A. O'Neil and I testified further about fraudulent activities of United States officials that affected Zuni lands.[398] For those interested in more recent and comprehensive work on the so-called Cruzate grants, see the work of Sandra Matthews-Lamb.[399]

It has been nearly twenty-five years since I wrote the manuscript that became this book. In that time, considerable historical scholarship has added to the body of knowledge about the Southwest and Zuni. Today I would probably not be so free with the word "frontier," which existed only in the minds of non-Zunis in the area. The work of Patricia Limerick and Richard White has broadened our understanding of what the old school called a frontier. At the same time, the earlier, extensive work of scholars like William H. Goetzmann remains highly helpful in analyzing the history of the West.[400]

I had the pleasure of getting to know the work of all three of these scholars while I directed the Institute of the American West. Later, when I became director of the Institute of the North American West, both White and Limerick, as well as Alvin M. Josephy, Jr., Floyd A. O'Neil, and Vine Deloria, Jr., provided important support, impetus, and perspective to my work in history during the 1980s and 1990s.

The translations from Zuni by Cushing and Baxter look romantic and stilted today, but more recent work by Jesse Green has helped to cement Cushing's place in the history of the Southwest.[401] Newer work by such scholars as David J. Weber[402] and John L. Kessel[403] has opened new vistas on the history of the Southwest. T. J. Ferguson has provided excellent new insights on the archaeology and prehistory of the A:shiwi.[404]

To put Lai-iu-ah-tsai-lu in perspective today, it is important to remember that, especially at Zuni, knowledge is power. Using his language and communication advantages, his leadership skills and religious positions in his tribal community, Lai-iu-ah-tsai-lu was certainly able to consolidate knowledge and achieve some political power. How much individual authority did Pedro Pino actually have? Probably not too much. Traditionally there was a careful balance of power between the priesthoods and the clans, the men controlling the priesthoods and the matriarchs presiding over the clans. Political leaders like Pino were watched closely by religious and clan leaders. He could not have made decisions that varied much from the consensus view in the community. Women's influence in the community, though not studied as intensely by Cushing and his peers, was strong.

While there may have been factionalism at Zuni, developing from those who favored or opposed a close relationship with the Americans, political organization seems to have worked well in the face of United States efforts to subjugate the Zuni people and culture. That's one reason the Zuni community is so strong today, in the twenty-first century.

And the community faces tough challenges today. A coal strip mine has been proposed and received permits to proceed in lands adjacent to the Zuni Salt Lake, in the area that has always been sacred and neutral, not only to Zuni but all the tribes in the region, Navajos and Apaches included. Today Zuni fears that this strip mine will do dire damage to the Salt Lake and is working hard to stop the mine or mitigate potential problems. Zuni also has not adjudicated its water rights, and that battle may be a crucial one for the future of the tribe.

I hope that this book helps the reader to understand the Zuni of the nineteenth century, Pedro Pino's Zuni, but also present-day Zuni and encourages support for the dynamic and robust Zuni culture which exists today. To a certain extent, I tried to write this book from a Zuni perspective. There is also a Navajo point of view, and many contemporary writers ably present that. Keep in mind that it was United States policy in the Southwest that directly led to the Navajo War. A broad understanding of Native American affairs and sovereignty issues today is important for all Americans. I hope this work adds to that understanding.

The author's royalties from this book will go to support the Zuni Senior Center in Zuni, New Mexico. I offer my heartfelt thanks to all those who helped me during the long preparation of this manuscript and book, especially the many Zunis whom I worked with over the years, including the late governor, Robert E. Lewis. I also offer my thanks to anthropologist T. J. Ferguson, John Alley and Barbara M. Bannon at Utah State University Press, Floyd A. O'Neil at the American West Center at the University of Utah, Elaine Thomas at Zuni, and the late Robert W. Delaney. Though I have had the pleasure to work with many great minds in western history, I am responsible for this work, of course, and any errors in either history or perspective are my own.

Appendix A
Biography of Pedro Pino
by
Frank Hamilton Cushing

Pedro Pino, or Lai-a-ai-tsai-luh [Lai-iu-ah-tsai-lu], must have been born some time during the last decade of the eighteenth century.[405] He is a member, on his mother's side, of the Keia-k-ia-li-kwe, or Eagle Gens, on his father's side, of the Sho-ho-i-ta-kwe, or Deer Gens [?].[406] He was distinguished in his early youth by remarkable strength and endurance, and, when only thirteen or fourteen years of age, he accompanied his father and uncle and other members of his tribe, on a war party against the Navajos, by whom he was at that time captured. For some reason or other the Navajos did not murder him. After living a year or two with them, during which period he suffered terribly, although he acquired a fair knowledge of the Navajo language, he was redeemed by a wealthy Mexican, named Pedro Pino, hence, this came to be his name. It seems that he remained with his Mexican friends for a considerable period, acquiring not only a fair foundation of the Spanish language from them, but also conceiving a great attachment for his foster father, Pedro Pino.

He was ultimately restored to his tribe by the latter, and, for three or four years, seems to have been, together with other now aged members of the tribe, kept rather closely under the severe discipline of a Spanish ecclesiastical school teacher. Full of life and mischief, he says himself that his education was of no benefit to him, that he ultimately rebelled against the rod and the master and left the Pueblo to dwell in the then occupied village of He-sho-ta, just north of the Valley of Zuni.

Between the ages of seventeen and eighteen he was probably married to the wife with whom he still faithfully lives.

At an early age he was made a member through an injury received in battle, of the order of Kea-shi-kwe, or Cactus People, a society of war surgeons, and one of the twelve secret sacred organizations of the tribe. Evincing, under the training of his father and uncles, remarkable prowess in war, he was made soon after this a member of the Priesthood of the Bow, and throughout his long life this prowess seems never to have forsaken him, and he ultimately became one of the highest members of the order.

In youth, a handsome man, with rare intellectual and executive ability, as well as one of the greatest orators of the tribe, he was early made a subchief. Through his connection with the sacred orders and by virtue of his clanship heredity, he became ecclesiastical head of the Eagle Gens, in addition to the sacred office of Keeper of the Gods of Prey, and the Medicine of the Hunt.

Through his sterling ability in council and his family connections, which were the wealthiest of the tribe, he was made, at this early age, Head Political Chief, an office which he occupied almost constantly during his forty-five subsequent years.

Through his connection with the Pino family and his early training with the Dominican priests, he had as a young man a remarkably good knowledge of Spanish, which circumstance gave him great consideration with the authorities in Santa Fe. He was personally well acquainted with and always well received by the last Spanish Governor of New Mexico, [Manuel] Armijo.

A prominent member of the Priesthood of the Bow, he was often the leader of war parties, which, from their success, attracted the attention and gained the favor of all other Pueblo Indians, as well as the Mexican authorities.

When the first expedition, after the close of the Mexican War, took place, Pedro Pino was still Head Chief of his nation, the hospitable host of the first Americans who ever officially visited his country, and chief of the first council which was held between his people and representatives of our government.

He became the staunch friend and powerful ally of General Kendrick, Campbell and other early officers of the Department of New Mexico, and he at present holds papers from nearly all officers of the United States Government who have visited his country since those early days. A few years since, when General Sherman, then a junior officer, passed through the country of Zuni, he was so impressed with the eloquence and ability of Pedro Pino, as to name him, in a letter which he gave the latter, the genius and intellect of Zuni.

Some six or eight years since, he was, after a brief term of rest, reelected to the office of Head Chief. He chose, however, only to name his son, Patricio Pino, or Pa-la-wah-ti-wa [Ba:lawahdiwa] as his successor. Although between eighty and ninety years of age, he has since then been constantly occupied with his agricultural pursuits, as well as with his duties as ecclesiastical chief of his clan, and Keeper of the Amulets of the Hunt.

During the early days of the Navajo wars and the subsequent War of Rebellion, he was promised, in reward for his services to our Government in both those enterprises, by the Commanding General then stationed at Santa Fe, opportunity for visiting the reverenced home of Washington, or of our Government. Through the intercession of brother priests, however, he was induced, on account of his connection with some religious ceremonials then to take place, to renounce the opportunity. During a period of more than thirty-one years he had occasionally renewed his hopes of visiting the East, or the "land of sunrise." Only a year or two since, feeling the influence of his increasing age and consequent infirmities, he at last gave up his long cherished hopes, and broke down in tears and sobs before me. It was, therefore, with remarkable alacrity, on my proposition of a journey with a chosen small delegation of the tribe, that he urged his claims to consideration. When reminded of his great age and infirmities, of the immense distance to be traveled over, and of the possible consequence of change in food and climate, he remarked;—"I have but a few days, as it were, to live. If disappointed, I must die ere the return of the pilgrims. If permitted to join your party, through the happiness of my heart and the joy of meeting my brothers of old Washington times, it may be I shall grow young again. Or, if I should die! What matters it? At best, I have but a few days to live."

It thus chanced that Pedro Pino was number[ed] among the Zuni visitors at Washington. During the protracted journey he suffered much, but with the rare fortitude which he had evinced during many a Navajo campaign, he endured his self-imposed sufferings and no word of complaint escape [*sic*] his lips from the beginning to the end of his long and novel journey.

Although aged, he was, during his brief residence in Washington, foremost spokesman of the little delegation; and while the other members of this delegation were absent with myself on the sacred pilgrimage to the Atlantic Ocean, under the influence of his host and hostess, Colonel and Mrs. Stevenson, he rapidly acquired and unfailingly observed the little niceties and usages of civilized society.

During his visit to the Tomb of Washington, at Mount Vernon, he was, while engage [*sic*] in prayer over the grave of the dead hero, most seriously affected, as he regarded Washington as the Great Cacique of all the American chiefs he had known during the prime of his life, and mourned that he should never have had an opportunity of grasping him by the hand.

While returning, the chill and damp of the journey gave him such a severe cold that he was taken violently ill on the following day; but with characteristic Zuni superstition and religious devotion, he remarked, in explanation of his illness;—"Before the grave of my father I stood in prayer, but my heart wept and my thoughts decayed, and illness entered therein." Whatever mat [*sic*] be the cause of Pedro Pino's illness, under any circumstance, he invariably ascribes it rather to supernatural causes than to the failing strength of years, hence he is sometimes known in his own tribe as the "old boy." He was intensely grieved on parting with his children, as he choses [*sic*] to call the present Head Chief and myself, but he endured the Journey back to his country with the same fortitude that had distinguished his outward trip, and arrived at his home by no means seriously ill from its effects.

F.H.C.

Appendix B
Orders No. 41 and Articles of Convention

[copy][407]

Winter Quarters Det.
Ill. Voltrs.
Camp mas [?] Zuni
July 1st 1848

Orders No. 41

The undersigned Lieutenant Colonel 1st Illinois Volunteers sent to the town of Zuni with instructions to Enforce the provisions of a treaty of Peace made on 20th of May Between the United States and the Navajo Indians which stipulates that there shall Be a Mutual Exchange of Prisoners and property, Captured By the People of New Mexico and the Pueblo Indians of the One Part and the Navajo Indians of the other part. Orders that the said town of Zuni shall immideatly [sic] Comply in Every particular with said treaty on their part, and that they shall from and after this Cease from mistreating said Navajo Indians who made said treaty either in person or [illegible] property.

IInd. The undersigned further notified said Pueblo de Zuni and its inhabitants that in Case of a Refusal on their part to comply with the provisions of said Treaty Between the Navajo Indians and the United States and in Case they refuse to obey the laws of the United States and New Mexico and the orders of the Commanding officer at Santa Fe then they will be treated as Enemeies [sic] of the United States and Troops in Sufficient

Numbers will be immideatly [sic] Marched against This Town to punish them for this refusal.

By order of

W.P. Boyakin Lt. Col. 1st

Ill. Voltrs. Camped [?] at Albyg [Albuquerque]
L Weywin [?]

_____ _____[?]

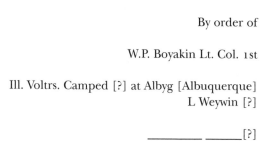

[copy]

Winter Quarters Detachments
1st Illinois Volunteers [?]
Pueblo de Zuni Upper California
this July 1st A. D. 1848

Articles of convention made and entered into by and between Lieutenant Col. W. P. Boyakin 1st Ill. Volunteers under instructions from and impowered by Col. Edward W. B. Newby, Commanding "L" Military Department of the United States of the first Part and the undersigned Governor and Military Commander of the Pueblo de Zuni of the second Part. Witnesseth the said part of the first Part stipulates and promises that the said Pueblo of Zuni shall Be Protected in the full management of all its rights of private Property and Religion. By the authorities Civil and Military of New Mexico and the United States.

Art. 2nd. The said Pueblo de Zuni through the undersigned Stipulates and agrees that hereafter until otherwise ordered said Pueblo shall in Every Particular obey strictly the Laws of the United States and the Territory of New Mexico and the orders of the Commanding officer of the Military forces in New Mexico.

Art. 3rd. The said first and several parties Mutually Stipulate and agree that they will for and on Behalf of the said United States and the Territory of New Mexico of the one part and the said Pueblo of Zuni of the other part Be and Remain good friends forever that they will always act towards Each other as Brothers.

Signed in Duplicate at said Camp on the day aforesaid in English by Both parties in presence of the undersigned.

W.P. Boyakin Lt. Col. 1st Ill. Voll. [*sic*]
for and on Behalf of the said party
of the 1st part

In Presence of
Capt. L. We. Adams [?] Ill. Voltrs.
Lt. Weywin [?] 1st Ill. Voltrs.

his
Pedro X Pino Governor of Pueblo de Zuni
mark

his
Antonio X Chapeton Commander of the War
mark   Parties of Zuni

Appendix C
Grant Given to Zuni, Year 1689

A t the town of Our Lady of Guadalupe del Paso del Rio del
Norte, on the twenty-fifty day of the month of September,
year one thousand six hundred and eighty-nine, His Excellency
the Governor and Captain General Don Domingo Jironza y Petroz
de Cruzate, declared before me that whereas within the reach of
his authority which he has in New Mexico and of his power over
the Queres Indians and over the apostates, and that after having
fought all the other Indians of the Pueblos, an Indian called
Bartolomé de Ojeda, who was the one who distinguished himself
most in battle succoring all points, surrendered himself finding
himself wounded by a gunshot and an arrow, and being already
disabled I ordered him to be taken and caused that they should
heal him with great care so that he might be examined and state
in his confession the condition in which is found the Pueblo of
Zuni and the other apostates of that Kingdom, and as the Indian
is versed in the Castillian language, is apt and can read and write,
and as he was the same who had conducted General Pedro de
Renero de Possada to that Pueblo, he being then on his way back
for this place and he being in the house of field marshal
Baninguas Mendoza, he was overtaken by the said Indian, and
being brought to my presence, I ordered that under oath he
declare what is his name and whether he is disposed to confess the
truth in so far as he might know and might be interrogated.

Questioned what is his name, where he is a native of, what is his
age and his occupation and whether he knows how Zuni is, he

stated that his name is Bartolomé de Ojeda and that he is a native
of the Province of New Mexico, at the Pueblo of Zia, and must be
twenty-one or twenty- two years of age, a little more or less, and
that he has not had any other occupation than the practice of agriculture, and that he knows how Zuni is, because he was an apos-
tate in that Kingdom, and thus he answers.

Questioned what are the boundaries which Zuni is known to have
on account of the crops it has on the Rio Teguella and whether the
Pueblo recognizes as its own because of having crops or because of
choice, and whether the Indians will again commit another infamy
[torn] other priests like the one they committed upon the custo-
dian priest [torn] the other priest whom they killed by shooting,
and the deponent answers no, that although it was true that all the
Pueblos had committed violence [torn] Priests of the Church and
that when the war was in Zia all the Indians were there, but that
with what had happened to them last year he judged it was impossible that they fail to give obedience, wherefore there were granted
by his Excellency the Governor and Captain General, Don
Domingo Jironza y Petroz de Cruzate, the boundaries that I here
state, On the north one league and on the East one league and on
the west one league on the south one league, and these being
measured from the four corners of the Pueblo and thus His
Excellency provided ordered and signed before me, the present
Secretary of State of War, to which I certify.

Domingo Jironza y Petroz de Cruzate
Before me
Pedro Ladron de Guitara
Secretary of State and War [408]

Appendix D
Treaty between the United States of America and Certain Indian Pueblos, or Towns

The following articles having been duly considered, and on behalf of the Government of the United States signed by the duly appointed Indian Agent, acting on a Commission, and on behalf of the respective pueblos, by the Governor and principal chiefs thereof who are duly authorized to act in their behalf, are binding on both parties to this Instrument.[409]

1. The contracting Pueblos do hereby place themselves under the exclusive jurisdiction and protection of the Government of the United States.

2. From and after the Signing of this Treaty the said Pueblos are bound and do hereby bind themselves, most solemnly, are never to associate with, or give countenance or aid to any tribe or band of Indians, or other persons or powers who may be, at any time, at [enmity] with the people of the United states; that they will, in all future time, submit, unconditionally, to said United States, and treat honestly and humanely every citizen thereof, and all other persons and powers at peace with the said States and that all cases of aggressions against the persons and interests of their respective Pueblos shall be referred [sic], for adjustment and settlement, to such tribunals as the Government of the United States has provided, or may provide.

3. The said Pueblos do hereby agree, that until it is otherwise provided, the laws now in force, and all others that may be passed, regulating the trade and intercourse, and for the

preservation of peace with the various tribes of Indians under the protection of the United States, shall be as binding and obligatory upon them as if said laws had been made for their sole benefit and protection, and that said laws may be duly enforced, and for all other useful purposes, their respective Pueblos shall be annexed [?] to such Individual [?] circuits or Districts as may be provided by the aforesaid Government.

4. The Government of the United States will, at its earliest convenience, afford to the contracting Pueblos its protecting power and influence; will adjust and settle, in the most practicable manner, the boundaries of each Pueblo, which shall never be diminished, but may be enlarged whenever the Government of the United States shall deem it advisable.

5. It is expressly understood and agreed by the contracting parties that the respective Pueblos are to be governed by their own laws and customs, and such authorities as they may prescribe, subject to the controlling power of the Government of the United States.

6. The Government of the United States will establish such agencies, at such time and in such places as the said Government may deem advisable for the protection and good management of the affairs of said Pueblos.

7. For and in consideration of their continued good conduct, the Government of the United States will grant to said Pueblos such donations, payments, and implements, and adopt such liberal and humane measures as said Government may deem just and proper.

In faith whereof, the undersigned have signed this Treaty, and affixed thereonto their seals, at Santa Fe, New Mexico, on the day and month included with their respective signatures, and in the year of our Lord one thousand eight hundred and fifty.

James S. Calhoun
Indian Agent residing at
Santa Fe, New Mexico
Acting as Commissioner
& on the part of the United
States. July 7th

Notes

Chapter One

1. The present location of Zuni was settled after the reconquest of New Mexico by Vargas in 1692. When the Zunis descended from their mesa, Dowa Yalanne, where they had been living defensively for some twelve years since the Pueblo Revolt, they consolidated most of their towns into one at the old site of Halona:wa, now called Iiwana (the Center Place). It had been on the opposite side of the river but was relocated to the side of the river where it currently stands. Actually, today the town has grown to encompass land on both sides of Zuni River, with buildings erected over the area of ancient Halona:wa. Frank Hamilton Cushing undertook archeological excavations of Halona:wa while he was there as a member of the tribe from 1879–1884. Later he joined the Hemenway Expedition of 1888–1890, which completed further excavations (Jesse Walter Fewkes, "Reconnaissance of Ruins on or near the Zuni Reservation," *Journal of American Ethnology and Archaeology* 1, part 2 [1891]: 103–4). For a history of one of the Zuni pueblos through the Spanish period to 1692, see Frederick Webb Hodge, *The History of Hawikuh* (Los Angeles: Hodge Publication Fund, 1937). For an outline of the remainder of the Spanish period, see Matilda Coxe Stevenson, "The Zuni Indians," in *Twenty-third Annual Report of the Bureau of American Ethnology, 1901–1902* (Washington, D.C.: GPO, 1904), 283–86.

2. Frank Hamilton Cushing, "The Discovery of Zuni or the Ancient Province of Cibola or the Seven Cities," handwritten manuscript, 1885, Frank Hamilton Cushing Manuscript Collection, MS.6.BOE.4.5, Southwest Museum, Los Angeles, California (hereafter cited as Cushing Collection, SWM).

3. Oakah L. Jones, Jr., introduction to *My Adventures in Zuni,* by Frank H. Cushing (Palmer Lake, Colo.: Filter Press, 1967; reprinted from *Century Magazine,* 1882–1883). For the best history of Zuni through this period and up to the present, see C. Gregory Crampton, *The Zunis of Cibola* (Salt Lake City: University of Utah Press, 1977). Also see Oakah L. Jones, Jr., *Pueblo Warriors and Spanish Conquest* (Norman: University of Oklahoma Press, 1966), as well as E. Richard Hart, ed., *Zuni and the Courts: A Struggle for Sovereign Land Rights* (Lawrence: University Press of Kansas, 1995) and T. J. Ferguson and E. Richard Hart, *A Zuni Atlas* (Norman: University of Oklahoma Press, 1985).

4. Will M. Tipton, "Memoranda of the Contents of the Spanish Archives in the Surveyor General's Office, at Santa Fe, New Mexico, That Relate to Lands of the Pueblo Indians," manuscript, 1911–1912, Reg. No. 75, 049, Denver Federal Records Center, Denver.

5. Frank Hamilton Cushing, "Biography of Pedro Pino," handwritten manuscript, n.d., MS.6.PP.4.1, Cushing Collection, SWM. This short document provides several interesting details concerning Pino's lineage, religious affiliation, and early life. (See Appendix A for the full text.)

6. Jones, *Pueblo Warriors,* 162.

7. Crampton, 53; Jones, *Pueblo Warriors,* 182–88.

8. Cushing, "Biography."

9. For the best presentation of this slavery argument, see Frank McNitt, *Navajo Wars: Military Campaigns, Slave Raids and Reprisals* (Albuquerque: University of New Mexico Press, 1972).

10. For a translation, see H. Bailey Carroll and J. Villasana Haggard, eds. and trans., *Three New Mexico Chronicles: The Exposicion of Don Pedro Bautista Pino, 1812; the Ojeada of Lic. Antonio Barreiro, 1832; and the Additions of Don José Augustin de Escudero, 1849.* (Albuquerque: Quivira Society, 1942).

11. Howard Roberts Lamar, *The Far Southwest, 1846–1912: A Territorial History* (New York: W. W. Norton and Company, 1970), 23–35.

12. Cushing, "Biography." The mission has recently been beautifully restored by the Catholic fathers.

13. For the most complete record of the ethnobotany of the Zunis, see Matilda Coxe Stevenson, "Ethnobotany of the Zuni Indians," in *Thirtieth Annual Report of the Bureau of American Ethnology,*

1908–1909 (Washington, D.C.: GPO,1915), 31–102. Other works deal with specific plants and localities and their use by the Zunis, e.g., V. L. Bohrer, "'Chinchweed' *(Pectes papposa)*, a Zuni Herb," *El Palacio* 64 (1957): 365. One source describing one of the various clays used by the Zunis and its locality is Edward S. Curtis, "Zuni," in *The North American Indian*, vol. 17, ed. F. W. Hodge (1926; reprint, New York: Johnson Reprint Corp., 1970), 102.

14. Two modern scholars have surmised that the lava beds were the natural boundary. Richard B. Woodbury says, "The barren lava flows that stretch south from Mount Taylor and the forests of the Zuni Mountains probably [formed] a natural boundary, one . . . between Acoma and Zuni." (Richard B. Woodbury, "The Antecedents of Zuni Culture," *Transactions of the New York Academy of Sciences*, 2d ser., 18, no. 6 [April 1956]: 556). Leslie Spier comments, "Along its [the Zuni Plateau's] eastern border extends the great lava bed, a sheet of desolate country separating the Zuni region from that of Acoma." (Leslie Spier, "Chronology of Zuni Ruins," in *Anthropological Papers of the American Museum of Natural History*, vol. 18 [New York: American Museum of Natural History, 1916], 215).

    More recent works provide ample evidence of Zuni boundaries. See Hart, *Zuni and the Courts,* and Ferguson and Hart, *A Zuni Atlas.*

    I have used, where possible, the spellings developed by the tribe and standardized in *A Glossary of Common Zuni Terms,* edited by Wilfred Eriacho and compiled by Richard Hart (Pueblo of Zuni: University of New Mexico Press, 1973).

15. Cushing speaks of Marata in several works, including "Discovery of Zuni," 61–63. Fewkes also mentions Marata. T. J. Fergusen, former director of the Zuni Archaeological Enterprise, has referred the author to Charles DiPeso's massive work on Casas Grandes (*Casas Grandes: A Fallen Trading Center of the Gran Chichimeca*, ed. Gloria J. Fenner, 3 vols. [Flagstaff, Ariz.: The Amerind Foundation, Inc./Dragoon/Northland Press, 1974]) and says that most archaeologists discount Fewkes's identification of Marata as Archeotekopa (Achiya: Dek'yapbow'a) but notes that DiPeso claimed the Zuni allied with a Chihuahuan tribe against Marata. Ferguson also points out that Spier has identified the Marata site.

16. Although the seminomadic existence of the Navajos creates some problems in determining their historical land-use patterns, some

documents shed light on the topic. Governor David Meriwether in 1854 said, "I find it very difficult to furnish you with a map of the country occupied by these tribes (Apaches, Navajos, and Utahs) as they never have any specific boundaries . . . and they claim all the lands not actually occupied by the whites." (David Meriwether to Commissioner of Indian Affairs, 29 September 1854, microfilm, letters received, New Mexico Superintendency, Record Group 75, National Archives). Undoubtedly, some Navajo families were allowed by the Zunis to settle early in their territory under Zuni law, but on the whole it was well into the 1860s, after the Navajos returned from Fort Sumner, before settlement to any great extent began in either the east, southeast, or south of Zuni by the Navajos. For an introduction to Navajo migrations, see Albert H. Schroeder, "Navajo and Apache Relationships West of the Rio Grande," *El Palacio* 70, no. 3 (fall 1963): 5–23, who says, "In 1850, Navajos were reported living to the right and Apaches to the left of the trail from Zuni to the Hopi villages, thus placing the Navajo area of occupation some distance north of the Little Colorado. Ten years later, Navajos averred they had never been to, or heard of, the Little Colorado; and Army patrols in that country could find no evidence of Navajo occupation"(13).

17. Some further sources which discuss the Province of Cibola and early Zuni history include Eugene Herbert Bolton, ed., *Spanish Exploration in the Southwest, 1542–1706* (New York: Barnes and Noble, Inc., 1908); George Parker Winship, "The Coronado Expedition, 1540–42," in *Fourteenth Annual Report of the Bureau of American Ethnology, 1892–1893* (Washington, D.C.: GPO, 1896); and Hodge, *History of Hawikuh.* The various towns and villages of the Zunis were known throughout the Spanish period by many different names. Hodge gives the best account of these in his *History* and in "Zuni" in the *Handbook of American Indians,* Smithsonian Institution, Bureau of American Ethnology Bulletin 30 (Washington, D.C.: 1910), 1015–20.

Cushing speculated that the word "Cibola" was a corruption of the word the Zunis used for themselves, Ashiwi or Shiwani, but that is unlikely. Cibola probably came from an Indian (perhaps Zuni) word and may have meant "buffalo," which it did come to mean to the Spaniards. It is noteworthy that southern tribes came to Zuni to trade for buffalo skins before and during the Spanish period (Frederick Hodge in *The Memorial of Fray*

Alonso de Benivides, translated by Edward E. Ayer and annotated by F. W. Hodge and Charles Fletcher Lummis [Albuquerque: Horn and Wallace Publisher, 1965], 269–70 n). Many other early Spanish chronicles mention Zuni as a trade center.

18. Among the many authorities who describe this aspect of Zuni life, see the following: Stevenson, "The Zuni Indians"; Cushing, *My Adventures in Zuni*; and Lieutenant A. W. Whipple, *Reports of Explorations and Surveys to Ascertain the Most Practicable and Economical Route for a Railroad from the Mississippi River to the Pacific Ocean, 1853–54,* 3rd Cong., 2d sess., 1854–56, S. Doc. 78, vol. 3.

19. Ruth L. Bunzel, "Zuni Ritual Poetry," in *Forty-seventh Annual Report of the Bureau of American Ethnology, 1929–1930* (Washington, D.C.: GPO, 1932), 675.

20. Ibid., 689.

21. Among the best are Ruth L. Bunzel, "Zuni Origin Myths," in *Forty-seventh Annual Report of the Bureau of American Ethnology, 1929–1930,* 545–609 and in the same volume Ruth L. Bunzel, "Introduction to Zuni Ceremonialism"; also Ruth Benedict, *Zuni Mythology,* 2 vols. (New York: Columbia University Press, 1935); Stevenson, "The Zuni Indians"; Dorothea C. Leighton and John Adair, *People of the Middle Place* (New Haven: HRAF Press, 1966); Frank Hamilton Cushing, *Zuni Folk Tales* (New York: Alfred A. Knopf, 1931); Frank Hamilton Cushing, "Outlines of Zuni Creation Myths," in *Thirteenth Annual Report of the Bureau of American Ethnology, 1891–1892* (Washington, D.C.: GPO, 1896), 449–62; Frank Hamilton Cushing, *Zuni Breadstuff,* Indian Notes and Monographs, vol. 8 (1920; reprint, New York: Heye Foundation, Museum of the American Indian, 1974); the translation by Dennis Tedlock from recitals by Andrew Peynetsa and Walter Sanchez, *Finding the Center* (New York: Dial Press, 1972); and probably most importantly, the Zunis' own *The Zunis' Self-Portrayals* (Pueblo of Zuni: University of New Mexico Press, 1972).

22. Bunzel, "Zuni Ceremonialism," 585.

23. Bunzel, "Zuni Origin Myths," 591.

24. Ibid.

25. Bunzel, "Zuni Ritual Poetry," 666–67.

26. Bunzel, "Zuni Origin Myths," 585.

27. Ibid.

28. Bunzel, "Zuni Ceremonialism," 481.

29. Bunzel, "Zuni Ritual Poetry," 709.

30. Bunzel, "Zuni Ceremonialism," 480.
31. Ibid.
32. Benedict, xxi
33. Bunzel, "Zuni Ritual Poetry," 666–67.
34. Bunzel, "Zuni Ceremonialism," 540.
35. Ibid., 478.
36. Ibid., 542.
37. Benedict, xxi.
38. Robert Glass Cleland, *This Reckless Breed of Men: The Trappers and Fur Traders of the Southwest* (New York: Alfred A. Knopf, 1963), 265; Joseph J. Hill, "Ewing Young in the Fur Trade of the Far Southwest, 1832–1835," *Oregon Historical Society Quarterly* 24, no. 1 (March 1923): 29–30; Alice B. Maloney, "The Richard Campbell Party of 1827," *California Historical Society Quarterly* 18, no. 4 (December 1939): 347–51; Frank Hamilton Cushing says, "When early in the present century [nineteenth] the first white men, Canadian and American trappers, penetrated to the Zuni country, they were well received and harbored from the Navajo" ("The Zunian Indians," manuscript, n.d., MS.6.BAE.4.20, Cushing Collection, SWM).
39. Frederick E. Voelker, "William Sherley (Old Bill) Williams," in *Mountain Men and Fur Traders*, ed. Leroy R. Hafen, vol. 8 (Glendale, Calif.: Arthur H. Clark Co., 1971), 374.
40. Hodge, *History of Hawikuh*, 40–42. Later in the sixteenth century, another Spaniard, the first governor of New Mexico, Juan de Oñate, heard of the Zuni Salt Lake. A member of the party visiting Zuni in 1598 reported, "The Governor sent Captain Farfan to see a saline which we heard was nine leagues from there. He returned on the third day, convinced that it must be the best saline in the world, and truly its salt would indicate this, for besides being exceedingly white and of marvelous grain, he said the saline was a league around, and that in the center of it there was a spring from which the saline was engendered, and therefore is very salty; that it has a depth of over a spear's length, and that in all of this depth, the salt forms a hardened crust, so that in order to extract the salt, it is necessary to use a bar or pickaxes" (Bolton, 235–36). There has been some dispute among non-Indian authors, among whom is Bolton, as to whether the Salt Lake was one or two days' travel from Zuni. It should be noted that the Zunis were famous for their swiftness of foot. There is a tradition that a Zuni on foot raced a horseback rider from St.

John's to Holbrook, Arizona, and won. Hodge said Zunis ran a twenty-five-mile, stick-kicking race in two hours (Frederick Webb Hodge, "A Zuni Foot-Race," *American Anthropologist* 3 [1890]: 227–31). *The Ogden (Utah) Junction* of 8 November 1873 reports the following: "Mr. Walker informed me at Camp Apache that he once made the distance between Zuni and Camp Apache, 120 miles, with a pair of good mules, in 60½ hours, but was beaten 2½ hours by an Apache, who left Zuni on foot at the same time with himself. He also offered to wager $500 that the same Indian could beat any horse or mule in Arizona for 340 miles. At such times, the Indians keep up a swinging gait or 'dog trot,' not relaxing their speed for a moment for, if need be, twenty-four hours. They run down deer in this manner" (p. 1, col. 5). Zuni tradition tells us that this was, in fact, one way the Zunis once hunted deer. Alfred Barnaby Thomas reveals that the Zunis' Salt Lake was also known to the Spaniards at the time of Governor Anza. He reports that Navajos chased a party of Gila Apaches to the lake (where they apparently took refuge in the "neutral" area) *(Forgotten Frontiers: A Study of Spanish Indian Policy of Don Juan Bautista de Anza, Governor of New Mexico, 1777–1787* [Norman: University of Oklahoma Press, 1932], 53). Many of the maps from this period clearly show the Zuni Salt Lake, including the famous Miera map of 1779 (Fray Francisco Atanasio Domínguez, *The Missions of New Mexico, 1776*, translated and annotated by Eleanor B. Adams and Fray Angelico Chavez [Albuquerque: University of New Mexico Press, 1956], 2–3, 200).

41. Sylvester Baxter, "The Father of the Pueblos," *Harpers's New Monthly Magazine* (June 1882): 79; F. W. Hill, "Navajo Salt Gathering," *University of New Mexico Bulletin* (Anthropological Series) 3, no. 4 (February 1, 1940): 5–25; Hill gives a full description of the Navajo tradition of salt gathering at the Zuni Salt Lake and elsewhere. Cushing, in "Outlines of Zuni Creation Myths," says, "When found by the Spaniards, the Zuni-Cibolans were still carrying on an extensive trade in this salt, which for practical as well as assumed mythic reasons they permitted no others to gather, and which they guarded so jealously that many of their later wars with the Navajos have been caused by slight encroachments on the exclusive right to the products of the lake to which the Zunis laid claim" (354). Stevenson, writing in 1901 in "The Zuni Indians," disputed this claim, saying, "It has been said that the Zunis claim the Salt Lake exclusively and

demand tribute from the other tribes, but such is not the case. In fact, the records tend to show that this locality has been from time immemorial the great source of salt supply for the Indians near and far. The writer has made careful inquiries on several occasions when the Hopi caravan stopped at Zuni on their return from the Salt Lake. The Zunis made no demand upon the Hopis whatever, but on the contrary, treated them as distinguished guests. The Navajos and Apaches collect the salt, although the lake is claimed as the special mother of each of the various tribes" (357). Late Zuni Governor Robert E. Lewis, in a personal conversation on 4 June 1973, supported Sevenson's argument, suggesting that the salt was free to everyone and the vicinity immediately around the lake was traditionally neutral, even in times of war. And even Stevenson reported that "many thrilling stories are told by the Zunis of their efforts in the past to anticipate the hated Navajos in reaching the lake, knowing that by so doing they would be preserved from harm" (357).

42. See *The Zunis' Self-Portrayals* for a few of their stories about hunting, including "Sacred Way to Hunt Deer," 6–7.

43. John G. Bourke, "Sacred Hunts of the American Indians," *International Congress of Americanists* 8 (1890): 357–68. Several beautiful rabbit sticks are in storage in the Zuni Collection at the Smithsonian Institution.

44. John G. Owens, "Some Games of the Zunis," *Popular Science Monthly* 39 (1891): 47.

45. John T. Hughes, *Doniphan's Expedition* (1848; reprint, Chicago: Rio Grande Press, 1962), 192–93.

Chapter Two

46. Fred Bowanie, ex-governor of Zuni, used almost exactly these phrases in describing the Zunis' land to me several years ago.

47. Frank Hamilton Cushing, "Biography of Pedro Pino," handwritten manuscript, n.d., Cushing Collection, SWM.

48. Sylvester Baxter, "The Father of the Pueblos," *Harpers's New Monthly Magazine*, June 1882, 87.

49. Ruth Falkenburg Kirk, "Southwestern Indian Jewelry," *El Palacio* 52, no. 2 (February 1945): 22.

50. For an introduction to the secular affairs of Zuni, see Watson Smith and John M. Roberts, *Zuni Law: A Field of Values*, Reports of the Rimrock Project Values Series, no. 4 (Millwood, N.Y.: Kraus Reprint Company, 1973).

51. E. Richard Hart, *The Zunis: Experiences and Descriptions,* with contributions from C. Gregory Crampton, Paul H. Norum, S. Lyman Tyler, and Sheila Bell (Pueblo of Zuni: University of New Mexico Press, 1973).

52. Cushing, "Biography."

53. Myra Ellen Jenkins, "Spanish Land Grants in the Tewa Area," *New Mexico Historical Review* 47, no. 2 (April 1972): 113–34; Myra Ellen Jenkins, "The Baltasar Baca 'Grant': History of an Encroachment," parts 1 and 2, *El Palacio* 68, no 1 (spring 1961) and no. 2 (summer 1961); Herbert O. Brayer, "Pueblo Indian Land Grants of the 'Rio Abajo,' New Mexico," *University of New Mexico Bulletin,* Historical Series 1, no. 1 (November 1, 1938); S. Lyman Tyler, *A History of Indian Policy* (Washington, D.C.: Bureau of Indian Affairs, 1973), 67–69.

54. Howard Roberts Lamar, *The Far Southwest, 1846–1912: A Territorial History* (New York: W. W. Norton and Company, Inc., 1970), 49–51.

55. George M. Wheeler, *Report upon United States Geographical Surveys West of the One Hundedth Meridian,* vol. 1 (Washington, D.C.: U.S. Geological Survey, 1889), 61.

56. Tilly E. (Matilda Coxe) Stevenson, *Zuni and the Zunians* (Washington, D.C.: n.p., 1881), 24. She reports a document in Pedro Pino's possession dated 1841. This document is now part of the collection housed at the Southwest Museum.

57. Cushing Collection, SWM.

58. Juan Christobal Armijo to Governor of Zuni, ca. 1875, MS.6.PP.1.1, Cushing Collection, SWM. Transactions included trading Zuni corn, or "grain," for brown sugar.

59. Lamar, 87, 90.

60. Cushing reports in "Biography": "When the first expedition, after the close of the Mexican War, took place, Pedro Pino was still Head Chief of his nation, the hospitable host of the first Americans who ever officially visited his country, and chief of the first council which was held between his people and representatives of our government."

61. Lamar. The author has relied heavily on Lamar's work for background material for the years from 1821 to 1846.

62. Frank McNitt, *Navajo Wars: Military Campaigns, Slave Raids and Reprisals* (Albuquerque: University of New Mexico Press, 1972), 101.

63. Ibid., 103 n.

64. John T. Hughes, *Doniphan's Expedition* (1848; reprint, Chicago: Rio Grande Press, 1962), 165.

65. Jacob S. Robinson, *Sketches of the Great West: A Journal of the Santa Fe Expedition, under Col. Doniphan, Which Left St. Louis in June, 1846* (Portsmouth, N.H.: Portsmouth Journal Press, 1848), 32.

66. McNitt, 121.

67. Hughes, 192–94.

68. Ibid.

69. Ibid.,194.

70. *Santa Fe Daily New Mexican*, 5 March 1886, p. 4, col. 2.

71. Elaine W. Higgins (depot historian), "The Bear Springs Story: A History of Ft. Wingate, McKinley County, New Mexico," manuscript, n.d., p. 4, Museum of New Mexico, Albuquerque; Hubert Howe Bancroft, *History of Arizona and New Mexico: 1530–1888* (San Francisco: The History Company Publishers, 1889), 423; McNitt, quoting Governor Bent, 122–23; Irving Telling, "New Mexico Frontiers: A Social History of the Gallup Area, 1881–1901" (Ph.D. diss., Harvard University, 1952), 2l; *Report of the Secretary of War, 30th Cong.,* 1st sess., 1848, S. Doc. 25, 9l; James H. Simpson, *Journal of a Military Reconnaissance from Santa Fe New Mexico to the Navajo Country Made in 1849,* edited and annotated by Frank McNitt (Norman: University of Oklahoma Press, 1964), xxx. McNitt quotes Captain W. M. D. McKissack as saying on February 16, 1847, "The Navajo Indians have broken their treaty and recommenced depredations."

72. McNitt, 124–26.

73. Frank Hamilton Cushing, "The Zunian Indians," manuscript, n.d., Cushing Collection, SWM.

74. Ralph Emerson Twitchell, *The History of the Military Occupation of the Territory of New Mexico from 1846 to 1851* (1909; reprint, Chicago: Rio Grande Press, 1963), 152; Simpson, 253, 254.

75. McNitt, 130 n.

76. W. P. Boyakin, "Orders No. 41," manuscript, in an envelope addressed to Pedro Pino, Zuni, New Mexico, 1848, MS.6.PP.1.5, Cushing Collection, SWM. (See Appendix B for the full text.)

77. W. P. Boyakin, "Articles of Convention," manuscript, 1 July 1848, Cushing Collection, SWM. (See Appendix B for the full text.)

78. Lieutenant A. W. Whipple, *Reports of Explorations and Surveys to Ascertain the Most Practicable and Economical Route for a Railroad from the Mississippi River to the Pacific Ocean, 1853–54,* 33rd Cong., 2d sess., 1854–56, S. Doc. 78, vol. 3, 73; Norman M.

Littell, "Proposed Findings of Fact in Behalf of the Navajo Tribe of Indians in the Area of the Overall Navajo Claim," Indian Claims Commission, Docket 229, 1967, vol. 5, reports, "In 1848 two large bodies of Navajo warriors attacked Zuni, one coming from the east and the other from the west" (1200).

79. Cushing, "Zunian Indians."

80. Annie Heloise Abel, *The Official Correspondence of James S. Calhoun* (Washington, D.C.: GPO, 1915), 21–23.

81. Ibid., 30; Robert V. Hine, *Edward Kern and American Expansion* (New Haven: Yale Press, 1962), 80.

82. Simpson, 118, 120, 124.

83. Richard H. Kern, "Notes of a Military Reconnaissance of the Pais de los Navajos in the Months of August and September, 1849," manuscript, 1849, no. 4274, Huntington Library, Pasadena, California.

84. Ibid.

85. Simpson, 120, 120 n.

86. Abel, 50–51; Colonel George Archibald McCall, *New Mexico in 1850: A Military View,* ed. Robert W. Frazer (1850; reprint, Norman: University of Oklahoma Press, 1968), 157.

87. Littell, 1201; McNitt, 159; Navajo Calendar (n.p., n.d.) says the Navajos "stole some animals and carried off many of their women."

88. Abel, 249–50.

89. Ibid.

90. Ibid.

91. McNitt, 165.

92. Abel, 250. The emphasis is Calhoun's.

93. Ibid, 237–46, emphasis added. The treaty was not ratified by Congress. (See Appendix D for the full text.)

94. Ibid., 260; Littell, 1201.

95. Abel, 263–64.

96. Richard H. Kern, Untitled diaries written while accompanying the Sitgreaves expedition of 1851, manuscript, 2 vols., no. 4277, Huntington Library, Pasadena, California.

97. Abel, 263–64.

98. McCall, 159, 159 n, 160–61; Abel, 274.

99. McNitt, 164, 166.

100. Ibid., 176, 289–90.

101. James S. Calhoun to Secretary of State, 30 June 1851, New Mexico Territorial Papers, National Archives; Littell, 1201–02.

102. Lamar, 94–96.
103. Kern, untitled diaries.
104. Chris Emmett, *Ft. Union and the Winning of the Southwest* (Norman: University of Oklahoma Press, 1965), 106.
105. Ibid.; Abel, 418; Kern, untitled diaries.
106. McNitt, 194–99.
107. Ibid.
108. Kern, untitled diaries; Captain Lorenzo Sitgreaves, *Report of an Expedition down the Zuni and Colorado Rivers*, 33rd Cong., lst sess., 1853, S. Doc. 59, 6.
109. McNitt, 198–99.
110. Electus Backus to Governor of Zuni, March 1852, MS.6.PP.1.2, Cushing Collection, SWM.
111. McNitt, 212–13.
112. Ibid., 206.
113. Tyler, 79.

Chapter Three

114. Electus Backus to Governor of Zuni, 17 May 1852, MS.6.PP.1.2, Cushing Collection, SWM.
115. Ibid.
116. Frank McNitt, *Navajo Wars: Military Campaigns, Slave Raids and Reprisals* (Albuquerque: University of New Mexico Press, 1972), 212–13; John Greiner, "The Journal of John Greiner," ed. Annie Heloise Abel, *Old Santa Fe* 3, no. 11 (July 1916): 207–9; Norman M. Littell, "Proposed Findings of Fact in Behalf of the Navajo Tribe of Indians in the Area of the Overall Navajo Claim," Indian Claims Commission, Docket 229, 1967, vol. 5, 1203, suggests that the Zunis killed the Navajo, but Greiner's journal seems to indicate, to this author, that the Apaches killed him.
117. Sylvester Baxter, "The Father of the Pueblos," *Harpers's New Monthly Magazine*, June 1882, 86.
118. Henry L. Kendrick to Sturgis, 26 April 1853, letters received (lr), Department of New Mexico (DNM), Records of Army Commands (RAC), Record Group (RG) 393, K-6, National Archives (NA).
119. Henry L. Kendrick to Sturgis, 2 May 1853, lr, DNM, RAC, RG 393, K-7, NA.
120. Henry L. Kendrick to Nichols, 6 November 1853, lr, DNM, RAC, RG 393, K-30, NA.

121. Henry L. Kendrick to Nichols, 2 December 1853, lr, DNM, RAC, RG 393, K-33, NA. All corn was purchased on the cob (Henry L. Kendrick to Jesup, 13 August 1855, Consolidated Correspondence File, Fort Defiance, RG 92, NA).

122. Henry L. Kendrick to Governor Pino, 20 November 1852, MS.6.PP.1.2.4, Cushing Collection, SWM.

123. Henry L. Kendrick to Sturgis, 10 May 1853, lr, DNM, RAC, RG 393, K-10, NA.

124. Henry L. Kendrick to Governor Pino, 25 May 1853, with attached note (offer of $30 for deserters), MS.6.PP.1.2.4, Cushing Collection, SWM; Henry L. Kendrick to Governor Pino, 20 May 1853, MS.6.PP.1.2.4, Cushing Collection, SWM reports sheep stolen by the Navajos. Henry L. Kendrick to Sturgis, 14 June 1853, lr, DNM, RAC, RG 393, K-15, NA reports several horses stolen from Zuni during a Navajo raid. McNitt, 227–28, reports Kendrick's dissatisfaction with policy.

125. Lieutenant A. W. Whipple, *Reports of Explorations and Surveys to Ascertain the Most Practicable and Economical Route for a Railroad from the Mississippi River to the Pacific Ocean, 1853–54*, 33rd Cong., 2d sess., 1854–56, S. Doc. 78, vol. 3, 61. Abbe Em. Domenech was also in the area during the 1850s. He, too, reported in 1860 that "formerly these Indians [the Navajos] boasted that they could exterminate all the Mexicans, and that if they did not do so, it was merely to save themselves the trouble of cultivating the maize and rearing flocks" (Abbe Em. Domenech, *Seven Years Residence in the Great Deserts of North America*, vol. 1 [London: Longman, Brown, Green, Longman, and Roberts, 1860], 207).

126. Baldwin Möllhausen, *Diary of a Journey from the Mississippi to the Coasts of the Pacific with a United States Government Expedition*, trans. Mrs. Percy Sinnett, vol. 1 (London: Longman, Brown, Green, Longman, and Roberts, 1858), 89.

127. Ibid; Ruth Falkenburg Kirk, "Southwestern Indian Jewelry," *El Palacio* 52, no. 2 (February 1945): 22, reported that the Zunis had traveled to Sonora to trade since the ninth century. It is understandable they would want a good trade route to the West Coast.

128. Müllhausen, 94, 99; Whipple, 67.

129. Möllhausen, 100; Whipple, 72; Lieutenant A. W. Whipple, Thomas Eubank, and William W. Turner, "Report upon the Indian Tribes," in *Report of Explorations . . . 1853–1854.*

130. S. D. Aberle, "The Pueblo Indians of New Mexico: Their Land, Economy and Civil Organization," *American Anthropologist Memoir* 70 (October 1948): 8.

131. Whipple, 71. Another account, likely by the same author, can be found in "Tribes of the Thirty-Fifth Parallel," *Harper's New Monthly Magazine,* September 1858, 458. Crampton identifies the host showing the papers to Whipple as Pedro Pino. Whipple calls him the "chief *cacique.*"As there was always some confusion among whites as to titles at Zuni in the early days, Crampton is possibly correct (C. Gregory Crampton, *The Zunis of Cibola* [Salt Lake City: University of Utah Press, 1977], 106).

132. "Report upon the Indian Tribes," 39–40. One then-popular theory suggested that the Pueblo peoples originated from the Aztecs. Whipple held this view and liberally translated Pino's remarks to support his theory (now known to have no basis in fact). Although the Zunis had few actual ditches, they and their Pueblo neighbors did have an extensive system of floodwater irrigation. For instance, see Ward Alan Minge, *Acoma: Pueblo in the Sky* (Albuquerque: University of New Mexico Press, 1976), 6–7, who reports eyewitness evidence of Acoma acequias in 1582.

133. Henry L. Kendrick to David Meriwether, 10 February 1854; Henry L. Kendrick to David Meriwether, 5 May 1854; Henry L. Kendrick to Ramon Luna, 18 December 1854; all are microfilm, letters received, New Mexico Superintendency, Record Group 75, National Archives (hereafter cited as lr, NMS, RG 75, NA).

134. David Meriwether to Commissioner of Indian Affairs, 29 September 1854, lr, NMS, RG 75, NA. Also "Meriwether Annual Report," 1 September 1854, NMS, RG 75, NA.

135. McNitt, 256–66.

136. Ibid., 267.

137. James H. Simpson, *Journal of a Military Reconnaissance from Santa Fe New Mexico to the Navajo Country Made in 1849,* edited and annotated by Frank McNitt (Norman: University of Oklahoma Press, 1964), 198–99; L. R. Bailey, *The Long Walk* (Los Angeles: Westernlore Press, 1964), 69. Bailey includes maps of the proposed treaty boundaries. *The Eighteenth Annual Report of the Bureau of American Ethnology, 1896–1897* (Washington, D.C.: GPO) also includes a map of treaty boundaries in plate 151.

138. McNitt, 267.

139. Ibid, 437.

140. Henry L. Kendrick to David Meriwether, 22 August 1856, lr, NMS, RG 75, NA.
141. Ibid.
142. Henry L. Kendrick to Pedro Pino, 20 May 1853, Cushing Collection, SWM.
143. Baxter, 86.
144. Joseph King Fenno Mansfield, *Mansfield on the Condition of the Western Forts*, edited and introduced by Robert W. Frazer (Norman: University of Oklahoma Press, 1963), 47 (roughly three thousand bushels a year). Henry L. Kendrick to David Meriwether, 13 June 1856, lr, NMS, RG 75, NA reports that Kendrick paid $1.35 a bushel for the corn from Zuni.
145. Kendrick to Meriwether, 13 June 1856.
146. Ibid.
147. Henry Dodge to David Meriwether, 13 June 1856, lr, NMS, RG 75, NA.
148. See Frederick Webb Hodge, *The History of Hawikuh* (Los Angeles: Hodge Publication Fund, 1937).
149. Deshkwi is "a yearly blessing ceremonial, for material and spiritual benefits. There are several forms, but generally these are occasions of self-imposed restrictions; for example a period when selling or trading is disallowed or a period when meals must not include meat" (*A Glossary of Common Zuni Terms*, edited by Wilfred Eriacho and compiled by E. Richard Hart [Pueblo of Zuni: University of New Mexico Press, 1973], 20).
150. Documents relating to the Dodge incident include the following: Howard Carlisle to Henry L. Kendrick (with note attached by Kendrick), 17 February 1857, lr, NMS, RG 75, NA; McNitt, 286–97; Enrique Dodge to Pedro Pino, 1855, MS.6.PP.1.15, Cushing Collection, SWM; "Examination of the Mexican Boy Who Joined Major Kendrick Near Zuni," November 1856, DNM, RAC 1850–1866, RG 393, NA; Henry L. Kendrick, "Orders No. 5," 3 February 1857, lr, DNM, RAC, RG 393, K-4/1, NA; Henry L. Kendrick to Howard Carlisle, 4 February 1857, lr, DNM, RAC, RG 393, K-4/2, NA; Henry L. Kendrick to Howard Carlisle, 8 February 1857, lr, DNM, RAC, RG 393, K-4/3, NA; Henry L. Kendrick to Nichols, 18 February 1857, lr, DNM, RAC, RG 393, K-3, NA.
151. Henry L. Kendrick to David Meriwether, 23 January 1857; Henry L. Kendrick, "Orders No.19," 12 April 1857, lr, DNM, RAC, RG 393, K-10/1, NA.

152. Henry L. Kendrick to David Meriwether, 23 January 1857, lr, NMS, RG 75, NA.

153. Frank Hamilton Cushing, "Biography of Pedro Pino," handwritten manuscript, n.d., Cushing Collection, SWM.

154. Henry L. Kendrick to David Meriwether, 11 February 1857, lr, NMS, RG 75, NA.

155. McNitt, 300–301.

156. Commissioner of Indian Affairs to James L. Collins, 14 July 1857; also letters of 8 August 1857 and 9 September 1857; all are lr, NMS, RG 75, NA; William Harley to James L. Collins, 1 January 1858, with enclosure of monthly report dated 1 November 1857; also monthly report dated 1 December 1857; all lr, NMS, RG 75, NA; Samuel M. Yost to James L. Collins, 1 December 1857, lr, NMS, RG 75, NA; William Harley to James L. Collins, 1 January 1858, lr, NMS, RG 75, NA. It is interesting to note that Harley said the "pueblos of Zuni"; that indicates that several of the farming villages were probably occupied during the period.

157. Harley to Collins, 1 January 1858; Yost to Collins, 1 December 1857.

Chapter Four

158. Ward Alan Minge, *Acoma: Pueblo in the Sky* (Albuquerque: University of New Mexico Press, 1976), 55.

159. Matt S. Meier and Feliciano Rivera, *The Chicanos* (New York: Hill and Wang, 1972), 106–7.

160. Ralph Emerson Twitchell, *The Spanish Archives of New Mexico*, vol. 1 (Grand Rapids, Mich.: Torch Press, 1914), 461–82.

161. *Annual Report of the Secretary of the Interior,* 36th Cong., lst sess., 1857, H. Doc., 564.

162. Ibid., 570.

163. Frank Hamilton Cushing, "Las Nutrias of the Zunis," 1893, MS.6.BOE.4.8, Cushing Collection, SWM. Carlos II ruled from 1665–1700. In the manuscript, Cushing reports "Onate" as the reconquerer, but it is clear what he means.

164. Ibid. Information on the Zuni tradition concerning the reconquest can be found in Matilda Cox Stevenson, "The Zuni Indians," in *Twenty-third Annual Report of the Bureau of American Ethnology, 1901–1902* (Washington, D.C.: GPO, 1904), 287–88, and Leo Crane, *Desert Drums* (Boston: Little, Brown and Co., 1928), 194. The last Navajo battle would have been in the late

1860s, possibly 1866. Pallé requested information from the Pueblo agency in 1880 about the grant and was told no records existed. Benjamin Thomas to Taylor F. Ealy, 24 August 1880, Copies of Miscellaneous Letters Sent, Pueblo Indian Agency, Denver Federal Records Center.

165. Stevenson, "The Zuni Indians," 354.

166. William E. Curtis, *Children of the Sun* (Chicago: The Inter-Ocean Publishing Co., 1883), 57–58.

167. Cushing, "Los Nutrias"; "Know All Men by These Presents," transcribed by William J. Oliver, at Blackrock, New Mexico, 26 August 1909, Entry 57, RG 75, Denver Federal Records Center; Hagberg to Olson, 7 November 1946, memorandum, Office of Indian Affairs, RG 75, NA.

168. Herbert O. Brayer, "Pueblo Indian Land Grants of the 'Rio Abajo,' New Mexico," *University of New Mexico Bulletin* (Historical Series) 1, no. 1 (November 1, 1938): 14–15; Ralph Emerson Twitchell, *The History of the Military Occupation of the Territory of New Mexico from 1846 to 1851* (1909; reprint, Chicago: Rio Grande Press, 1963), 455, reported that the Indian who is allegedly being questioned in the account of the grant, Bartolomé de Ojeda, actually led an attack of Spaniards on the pueblo of Jemez and was praised for his gallantry. Minge, 25, suggests that a Governor Cruzate did penetrate New Mexico territory in 1688 and sacked the pueblo of Zia and that the existing Cruzate grant to Acoma is a poor copy of a legitimate deed.

169. Twitchell, *History of the Military Occupation*, 477–83; Lansing B. Bloom, *Antonio Barreiro's Ojeada Sobre Nuevo Mexico*, Historical Society of New Mexico Publications in History, vol. 5 (Santa Fe: El Palacio Press, 1928). The title of Barreiro's book is found verbatim in one grant. Minge also points out the unlikelihood of Ojeda's memory: "He of the remarkable memory for grant boundaries" (56).

The Spanish reconquest of Zuni did not take place until 1692, while the Cruzate grants seem to indicate that event occurred in 1688 (at least there was limited action against Zia). It is interesting that the document reports a question as to what land the pueblo itself claims. Then the grant issues four square leagues to the pueblo. Had the Zunis lost their rights through the uprising, perhaps a document such as this one might have been necessary to reaffirm the status of the pueblo under Spanish law, with the minimum grant of four square leagues authorizing them to use what lands they could, as Spanish law prescribed.

170. *Annual Report of the Commissioner of General Land Office* (Washington, D.C.: GPO, 1876), 242–43.

171. In the 1890s, Will M. Tipton did a thorough investigation of the Pueblo land grants. He commented on the Zuni papers: "There are two Spanish papers in this case. The one dated 1689 is spurious" (Twitchell, *History of the Military Occupation,* 483). If, by this statement, Tipton meant that there was a second Spanish paper which was not dated 1689, it is not in the archives today. Obviously a good deal of mystery surrounds the origin of the Cruzate papers.

172. "Zuni, Bureau of Land Management, Santa Fe, N.M.," Pueblo land grant papers, case 5, papers 19–25, New Mexico Archives, Santa Fe.

173. Ibid., papers 15–17. During the years between the Pueblo Revolt and the reconquest, the Zunis maintained a defensive retreat village on top of the mesa but continued to farm and carry out normal activities throughout the rest of their territory.

174. *Survey of Lands Claimed by the Zuni Pueblo Indians, New Mexico and Issuance of Patent Therefore,* 71st Cong., 3rd sess., 1931, S. Rept. 1780, 2–3.

175. Ibid., 3–4.

176. *Annual Report of the Department of the Interior, 1899* (Washington, D.C.: GPO, 1899), xlvii. Of course, the Zunis had actually had the land in their possession for centuries longer than the two cited by the secretary of the interior.

177. *Annual Report of the Secretary of the Interior, 1900,* 56th Cong., 2d sess., 1900, H. Doc., 172.

178. *Confirming Title to Certain Land to Indians in New Mexico,* 56th Cong., 1st sess., 1900, H. Rept. 1571.

179. *Annual Report of the Department of the Interior, 1901* (Washington, D.C.: GPO, 1901), liv.

180. *Annual Report of the Commissioner of Indian Affairs, 1901–1902,* 57th Cong., 1st sess., 1901, Serial Set 4290, 166. H.R. 8316 was entered by the 57th Cong., 1st sess.

181. Meier and Rivera, 106–7.

182. "Survey of Lands Claimed," 2–3. Public Law 825 was enacted March 3, 1931, during the 71st Cong., 3rd sess.

183. "Zuni, Bureau of Land Management," paper 54. The note also states that Leopoldo J. Eriacho "was in and examined papers of the Zuni Pueblo."

184. S. Lyman Tyler, *A History of Indian Policy* (Washington, D.C.: Bureau of Indian Affairs, 1973), 68.
185. Brayer, 25. Brayer also points out that the Sandoval decision did not end the Pueblos' problems. Every means available was used to get Pueblo lands throughout the early years of the twentieth century. Albert B. Fall and Senator Holm O. Bursum tried sophisticated legislative means to take Pueblo lands, but the Pueblos and their allies endured, and finally the Pueblo Lands Act of 1924 gave them some stability in land ownership.

Chapter Five

186. *Wagon Road from Fort Defiance to the Colorado River,* 35th Cong., lst sess., 1857–58, H. Doc. 124, 39.
187. W. Turrentine Jackson, *Wagon Roads West* (New Haven: Yale University Press, 1965), 245–47.
188. *Wagon Road from Fort Defiance,* 39.
189. Ibid., 84–85.
190. John Udell, *John Udell Journal,* with an introduction by Lyle H. Wright (Los Angeles: N. A. Kovach, 1946), 24–25.
191. Ibid., 58–59
192. Ibid.
193. Ibid.
194. Ibid.
195. Dixon Stansbury Miles to Wilkins, 15 October 1858 (with enclosures), lr, DNM, RAC, RG 393, M-73, NA.
196. Udell, 58–59.
197. William P. Floyd, journal kept from 27 September 1858 to 1 May 1859 during Beale's expedition, typewritten copy, manuscript 19334, p. 35, Huntington Library, Pasadena. In April 1858, government agents dissuaded Zia, Santa Anna, Jemez, and Laguna from forming a retaliatory war party against the Navajos and then in September reported that conflict was imminent between the Navajos and the United States. John Ward to Samuel M. Yost, 9 April 1858 and 24 August 1858, lr, NMS, RG 75, NA.
198. Samuel M. Yost to Editor of *Santa Fe Weekly Gazette,* 24 September 1858, enclosed in a letter of Governor to Secretary of State, 16 October 1858, New Mexico Territorial Papers, National Archives.
199. Miles to Wilkins, 15 October 1858.
200. Frank McNitt, *Navajo Wars: Military Campaigns, Slave Raids and Reprisals* (Albuquerque: University of New Mexico Press, 1972), 346; Letter of 17 October 1858, lr, DNM, RAC, RG 393, M-79, NA.

201. Dixon Stansbury Miles to Wilkins, 23 October 1858, with enclosure from Lane to Lane, 22 October 1858, lr, DNM, RAC, RG 393, M-75, NA. McNitt interpreted the documents to mean that the Zunis left the troops behind and therefore burned the village alone (without the U.S. troops) and that the Zunis' capture of Navajo ponies was all that the campaign accomplished (McNitt, 347).

202. McNitt, 347, 353–62; Governor to Secretary of State, 29 November 1858, New Mexico Territorial Papers, National Archives.

203. *Wagon Road—Ft. Smith to the Colorado River,* 36th Cong.,1st sess., 1859–60, H. Doc. 42, 36. Beale said he hoped the "Indians [are] in a selling humor. In this respect all Indians are singular. They either sell readily and for little or nothing, or not at all, and are as capricious in their dispositions as possible." Certainly the Zunis had good reason to terminate the trade relationship with the U.S. But this was not the case. If there was any real reason for Beale to worry, it would have come from word that the Zunis periodically had a religious observance called Deshkwi. During this time, Zunis are required either to give their goods away or refrain from dealing altogether.

204. Floyd, 28.

205. *Wagon Road—Ft. Smith to the Colorado River,* 36–40.

206. Ibid., 40.

207. Edward F. Beale to Pedro Pino, 28 March 1859, MS.6.PP.1.3, Cushing Collection, SWM.

208. McNitt, 366.

209. Norman M. Littell, "Proposed Findings of Fact in Behalf of the Navajo Tribe of Indians in the Area of the Overall Navajo Claim," Indian Claims Commission, Docket 229, 1967, vol. 5, 1208.

210. Alexander Baker to James L. Collins, 14 August 1859, lr, NMS, RG 75, NA.

211. Captain J. G. Walker and Major O. L. Shepherd, *The Navajo Reconnaissance,* with foreword, annotations, and index by L. R. Bailey (Los Angeles: Westernlore Press, 1964), 105–6.

212. Henry L. Kendrick to O. L. Shepherd, 25 October 1859, lr, NMS, RG 75, NA.

213. O. L. Shepherd to James L. Collins, 3 May 1859, lr, NMS, NA; Samuel M. Yost to James L. Collins, 6 February 1859, lr, NMS, NA.

214. Ibid.
215. Ibid.

Chapter Six

216. Fort Fauntleroy was founded at Ojo del Oso. In 1861, when Col. Fauntleroy joined the Confederate forces in the Civil War, the fort was renamed Fort Lyon. The fort was nearly abandoned during the Civil War, but a post did remain during those years as a mail depot. Fort Wingate was established in 1862 at Ojo del Gallo, near the present site of San Rafael. In 1868 it was abandoned, and the new Fort Wingate was established at Ojo del Oso on the original site of Forts Lyon and Fauntleroy. (Robert W. Frazer, *Forts of the West* [Norman: University of Oklahoma Press, 1965], 168; Francis Paul Prucha, *A Guide to the Military Roots of the United States, 1789–1895* [Madison: State Historical Society of Wisconsin, 1964], 117, 71, 64, 86).

217. *Annual Report of the Commissioner of Indian Affairs, 1860* (Washington, D.C.: George W. Bowman, Printer, 1860), 165–67.

218. Ibid. There is no reason to believe that "designing Mexicans" sowed the seeds of these thoughts with the Pueblo leaders. It may be instructive to examine two examples of Anglo leaders' prejudice and condescension toward both the Mexican American and Indian population in the territory during this period and indeed throughout the nineteenth century. Certainly these attitudes molded current policy to some extent. The "American" view can best be represented by quoting from two reports during the 1890s. Dr. Daniel Dorchester investigated Zuni schools in 1892. "Linking them with the old idolatrous Canaanites of earliest recorded history," Dorchester branded the Zuni religion as "fetishism of the grossest kind, complicated with all natural phenomena, and the atmospheric elements are its symbols. It places animals on an equality with mankind. Sometimes recognizing them as man's superiors. This religion assumes man's utter helplessness within the natural realm . . . . Do we wonder at his lack of truthfulness, consistency and moral consciousness?" (Dr. Daniel Dorchester, "Report of the Superintendent of Indian Schools," *Report of the Secretary of the Interior,* 52nd Cong., 2d sess., 1892, H. Doc., Serial Set 3088, 527–63).

This attitude was not reserved for the Indians of New Mexico. In another report, in 1897, the Indian agent to the Pueblo

Indians in New Mexico revealed his attitude toward a trial and its
Mexican American jury: "I distrust the outcome of these pro-
ceedings. Based upon former experience, there is no foundation
to expect that salutary results will follow this prosecution. The
petit jury, speaking algebraically, is, in any community, however
enlightened, nearly always an unknown quantity, represented by
X; it is even more uncertain, composed of the Mexican-
American citizen, commonly referred to as 'a greaser' who, by
years of intimate association with the Indians, has imbibed more
or less sympathy with his religious tenets . . . . Interfere with what
your average Mexican is pleased to call his 'religion,' and he
immediately becomes aroused to the highest pitch of fanaticism,
capable of undergoing any sacrifice, any hardship." ("Annual
Report of C. E. Nordstrom of 1897," Copies of Miscellaneous
Letters Sent, Pueblo Indian Agency, Denver Federal Records
Center). The jury report was published in the *Report of the
Governor of New Mexico to the Secretary of the Interior, 1897*
(Washington, D.C.: GPO, 1897), 84, found in the New Mexico
Archives, Santa Fe. But the secretary of the interior and the gov-
ernor of New Mexico found the passage so offensive that pieces
of cardboard were pasted over it (*Report of the Governor of New
Mexico, 1897*, p. 442, New Mexico Archives, Santa Fe). The pas-
sage was also deleted from the agent's report when published in
the *Annual Report of the Secretary of the Interior, 1897*.

219. *Annual Report of the Commissioner of Indian Affairs, 1860*, 165–67.
220. E. S. Canby to Assistant Adjutant General (AAG), 20 February
      1861, lr, DNM, RAC, RG 393, C-33, NA; E. S. Canby to AAG, 25
      January 1861, lr, DNM, RAC, RG 393, C-22, NA; E. S. Canby to
      AAG, 4 February 1861, lr, DNM, RAC, RG 393, C-23, NA.
221. Information on Zuni/U.S. relations from 1859–1861, can be
      found in the following: Frank McNitt, *Navajo Wars: Military
      Campaigns, Slave Raids and Reprisals* (Albuquerque: University of
      New Mexico Press, 1972), 382–433; Norman M. Littell,
      "Proposed Findings of Fact in Behalf of the Navajo Tribe of
      Indians in the Area of the Overall Navajo Claim," Indian Claims
      Commission, Docket 229, 1967, vol. 5, 1208–9; *Annual Report of
      the Commissioner of Indian Affairs, 1860*. In *Navajo Calendar* (n.p.,
      n.d.), Lieutenant Telford, 17 October 1860, reports that in
      October of 1860 a Navajo woman said that Zarcillos Largos had
      recently been killed by a war party of Zunis near Canyon de
      Chelly. Largos was a prominent Navajo leader.

Also see Laws to Rich, 16 January 1860 [*sic,* 1861], lr, DNM, RAC, RG 393, C-34, NA; E. S. Canby to AAG, 6 January 1861, lr, DNM, RAC, RG 393, C-11, NA; E. S. Canby to McFerren, 22 November 1860, lr, DNM, RAC, RG 393, NA; Laws to Rich, 16 December 1860, lr, DNM, RAC, RG 393, C-12, NA.

222. Howard Roberts Lamar, *The Far Southwest, 1846–1912: A Territorial History* (New York: W. W. Norton and Company, Inc., 1970), 116; E. S. Canby to Pedro Pino, 16 January 1861, MS.6.PP.1.9, Cushing Collection, SWM.

223. Frank Hamilton Cushing, "Biography of Pedro Pino," handwritten manuscript, n.d., Cushing Collection, SWM.

224. Electus Backus to AAG, 7 May 1862, RAC, 1850–1866, RG 393, RRLA, NA; Canby to AAG, 19 February 1861, lr, DNM, RAC, RG 393, C-32, NA.

225. Albert Pfeiffer to Pedro Pino, 18 October 1863, MS.6.PP.1.32, Cushing Collection, SWM; Lamar, 116.

226. Littell, 1209.

227. Campbell to [?], 21 August 1863, DNM, RAC, 1821–1920, RG 393, NA; Kit Carson to Cutler, 19 August 1863, lr, DNM, RAC, 1821–1920, NA; Kit Carson to Adjutant General (AG), 24 July 1863, lr, DNM, RAC, 1821–1920, NA; Chacon to Holmes, 30 June 1863, lr, DNM, RAC, 1821–1920, 1862, NA.

228. Hargrave to Commanding Officer, Fort Wingate, 10 September 1863, DNM, RAC, 1821–1920, RG 393, NA; Chavez to Cutler, 17 September 1863, DNM, RAC, 1821-1920, RG 393, NA.

229. Lamar, 123–24; Anderson to PA, Fort Wingate, 5 July 1864, lr, DNM, RAC, RG 393, 149-E-97, NA.

230. Joseph H. Eaton to Captain, 6 July 1864, lr, DNM, RAC, RG 393, 149-E-97, NA.

231. Joseph H. Eaton to Pueblo of Zuni, 10 August 1864, MS.6.PP.1.18, Cushing Collection, SWM.

232. Joseph H. Eaton to Cutler, 15 September 1864, lr, DNM, RAC, RG 393, 156-E-132, NA; Joseph H. Eaton to Cutler, 21 October 1864, lr, DNM, RAC, RG 393, 161-E-152, NA.

233. Lamar, 125; *Annual Report of the Secretary of the Interior, 1865,* 39th Cong., lst sess., H. Doc., Serial Set 1248, 356; Joseph P. Naysure and Henry M. Benson to Pedro Pino, 22 August 1864, MS.6.PP.1.30, Cushing Collection, SWM; George M. Milling to Pedro Pino, 22 February 1864, MS.6.PP.1.28, Cushing Collection, SWM.

234. McNitt, in *Navajo Wars,* points out that some private expeditions against the Navajos had the slave trade as their primary objective.

235. Shaw to Cutler, 16 May 1865, lr, DNM, RAC, RG 393, S-149, NA.

236. Shaw to Cutler, 25 May 1865, lr, DNM, RAC, RG 393, S-150, NA.

237. Littell, 1211; Shaw to [?], 1 August 1865, in *Navajo Calendar.*

238. Ibid.

239. Gerald Thompson, *The Army and the Navajo: The Bosque Redondo Reservation Experiment, 1863–1868* (Tucson: University of Arizona Press, 1976), 87–88.

240. Butler to James H. Carleton, 12 July 1866, lr, DNM, RAC, RG 393, B-154, NA.

241. Littell, 1211.

242. John S. Crouch and French to Pedro Pino, 1 June 1866, MS.6.PP.1.13, Cushing Collection, SWM; French to Pedro Pino, 22 October 1866, MS.6.PP.1.20, Cushing Collection, SWM; John S. Crouch to PA, 21 June 1866, lr, DNM, RAC, RG 393, B-137, NA; Butler to Forrest, 28 July 1866, lr, DNM, RAC, RG 393, B-164, NA.

243. Ward Alan Minge, *Acoma: Pueblo in the Sky* (Albuquerque: University of New Mexico Press, 1976), 81 and 81 n, reports that the Spanish canes, according to Myra Ellen Jenkins, date back at least to the eighteenth century and perhaps earlier. The Lincoln canes were dated 1863 and inscribed, "A. Lincoln, Pres. U.S.A.," although they were brought back from Washington by Superintendent Michael Steck in May 1864.

244. Frank D. Reeve, ed., *Albert Franklin Banta: Arizona Pioneer*, Historical Society of New Mexico Publications in History 14 (Albuquerque, 1953), 1–3, reports that Banta was born in 1843, arrived in Arizona Territory in 1863, and was also known as Charles Franklin. Banta wrote the manuscript from memory when he was seventy-five. Reeve first published the account in the *New Mexico Historical Review* 27 (1952).

245. Ibid., 30.

246. Ibid. "Being unaware of the danger of eating meat during the prohibited time, of course I ate my usual allowance of broiled mutton. The little children stared at me in wonder while I ate the meat, no doubt looking to see me topple over dead. The older people gravely shook their heads but said nothing. Strange to relate in two days I was taken down sick, and had the worst spell of sickness any one could have and recover. The nature of my sickness I never knew" (32).

247. Ibid., 30. Banta uses the term *tah-poop,* which is a version of the Zuni word for governor of the tribe. He also reported that another member of the Zuni delegation was war captain

Salvadore. Salvadore was also mentioned as war captain in 1857 (*A Glossary of Common Zuni Terms,* edited by Wilfred Eriacho and compiled by Richard Hart [Pueblo of Zuni: University of New Mexico Press, 1973], 21).

248. Traditionally Zunis breathe a prayer onto the hand in conjunction with the handshake, which is a religious ceremonial gesture.

249. Reeve, 34. Following his adoption, Banta wrote that he considered the pueblo his home and the Zunis his people.

250. Banta repeats an interesting theory concerning peace with the Apaches: "For centuries these people were on the defensive against hostile tribes—coyotes, they call them—and in my time with them we had much trouble with the Navajos. A tradition of the Zunis says that more than two hundred years ago, they were attacked by a large body of Apaches, but at night the Apaches withdrew a short distance from the walls. One morning the priest, as was his custom, was walking along the edge of the wall and was shot dead by an Apache who had hidden behind a rock near the wall. The dead priest fell off and that night the Apaches carried the body to their camp. Having stript [*sic*] the body of clothing, to their great astonishment the body was white something unknown and unheard of by them. Being superstitious and curiosity so great to find out the meaning of the white skin, the Apaches proposed a council of peace which was excepted [*sic*] by the Zunis. The Zunis took advantage of the situation and told the Apaches the white skin was a superior being, that he would live again, and much more to the same effect. The Apaches then proposed a lasting peace; as the white skin was to live again they desired to see him. This peace pact has remained inviolate up to the present day. In corroboration of this tradition I cite Spanish history which says: 'En 1672 se declarraron en guerra los Apaches, invadiendo el pais, y Aguias, pueblo de los Zunis, donde fue asesinado por ellos, en October 7 de 1672, fray Pedro de Ayala . . . .'" Reeve points out that "I have not been able to locate the source of this quotation, but the substance of it is historically correct. The Apache did raid Zuni pueblo and kill Fr. Pedro de Avila y Ayala, October 7, 1672" (Ibid., 38–39). See Frederick Webb Hodge, *The History of Hawikuh* (Los Angeles: Hodge Publication Fund, 1937).

251. Reeve, 39. Banta has been accused of trying to upstage Frank Hamilton Cushing with his claim of being offered a position in the Priesthood of the Bow.

252. Ibid., 40
253. Lawrence C. Kelly, *The Navajo Indians and Federal Indian Policy: 1900–1935* (Tucson: University of Arizona Press, 1968), 6–7.
254. Michael Steck to Commissioner of Indian Affairs, 2 February 1864, lr, NMS, RG 75, NA reports an estimate for the cost of surveys of Laguna, Acoma, and Zuni. This indicates the superintendent had either a knowledge of Zuni's grant or was thinking about a reservation for the tribe, but it was more than ten years before the Zunis' grant was delivered to the New Mexico surveyor general, and more than ten years more before any action was taken toward establishing a reservation.

Chapter 7

255. *Annual Report of the Secretary of Interior, 1868*, 40th Cong., 3rd sess., H. Doc., 621.
256. Ibid., 638; Howard Roberts Lamar, *The Far Southwest, 1846–1912: A Territorial History* (New York: W. W. Norton and Company, Inc.,1970), 137–70. Elkins was then New Mexico's district attorney. For a short biography, see William A. Keleher, *Maxwell Land Grant* (New York: Argosy-Antiquarian Ltd., 1964), 147–49.
257. Frank Hamilton Cushing, "Los Nutrias," manuscript 92, chapter 4, Cushing Collection, SWM.
258. *Annual Report of the Secretary of the Interior, 1869–1870*, 41st Cong., 2d sess., 691.
259. *Annual Report of the Secretary of the Interior, 1868*, 636.
260. *Annual Report of the Secretary of the Interior, 1869–1870*, 693.
261. *Annual Report of the Secretary of the Interior, 1870*, 41st Cong., 3rd sess., 1870, 626.
262. A. W. Evans to Pedro Pino, 26 July 1869, MS.6.PP.1.19, Cushing Collection, SWM.
263. Frank D. Reeve, ed., *Albert Franklin Banta: Arizona Pioneer*, Historical Society of New Mexico Publications in History 14 (Albuquerque, 1953), 37–38.
264. *Weekly New Mexican*, 9 November1869, p. 2, col. 2.
265. Brown to Pedro Pino, 17 April 1870, MS.6.PP.1.7, Cushing Collection, SWM.
266. W. F. M. Arny, *Indian Agent in New Mexico: The Journal of Special Agent W. F. M. Arny, 1870*, with an introduction and notes by Lawrence R. Murphy (Santa Fe: Stagecoach Press, 1967), 31–32.
267. W. F. M. Arny to Pedro Pino, 26 June 1870, MS.6.PP.1.35, Cushing Collection, SWM.

268. William Redwood Price to Pedro Pino, 3 June 1870, MS.6.PP.1.35, Cushing Collection, SWM.

269. Henry W. Dodd and Coleman F. Ludlum to Pedro Peno [*sic*], 18 April 1869, MS.6.PP.1.27, Cushing Collection, SWM; Reeve, 40–41.

270. John S. A. Clark and John H. Farrand to Pedro Pino, 25 May 1870, MS.6.PP.1.11, Cushing Collection, SWM.

271. *Annual Report of the Commissioner of Indian Affairs, 1871* (Washington, D.C.: GPO, 1872).

272. Ibid. This report also contains the following account, judged by this author to be apocryphal: "For many years these Indians [Navajos and Zunis] were at war with each other, and in 1863, the Zuni Indians had about one hundred Navajo captives. Finding it too expensive to feed them, they decided to 'give them a chance for their lives and liberty.' Alas! but a poor chance. This town is constructed with houses from five to seven stories high, streets and alley-ways narrow, and difficult to find a way out unless well acquainted with them. In the public square of this town the Zuni Indians placed their captive Navajos and told them to escape, if they could. At each corner were placed a couple of Zuni warriors, armed with clubs and knives; and the Navajos attempted to escape, but not one got out of the town alive. Their own description of this massacre made me shudder and filled my mind with horror" (590).

George Gwyther, "The Pueblo Indians," *Overland Monthly* 6 (1871): 269, contains a similar account which gives the date of this alleged occurrence as 1866 and claims that 160 Navajo men, women, and children were pushed off a cliff. Both stories must have originated from the same account. Both were published in 1871, and no contemporary account of this occurrence exists, nor does any account suggest that the story may have a basis in fact. The reports are certainly inconsistent with both other accounts of the period and the character of the Zuni people.

273. Norman M. Littell, "Proposed Findings of Fact in Behalf of the Navajo Tribe of Indians in the Area of the Overall Navajo Claim," Indian Claims Commission, Docket 229, 1967, vol. 5, 1212; W. F. M. Arny to [?], 31 May 31, 1871, *Navajo Calendar* (n.p., n.d.).

274. *Report to the Secretary of War,* 41st Cong., 3rd sess., 1870, H. Doc. 1, part 2, 15.

275. Reeve, 220.

276. Reeve reported that "Solomon Barth was a prominent citizen of northern Arizona. He arrived in Arizona as early as 1860; moved to the Prescott region in 1863; located at St. Johns in 1873, first settled the previous year . . . . He was a member of the 11th Legislative Assembly . . . . He was convicted for fraud in connection with the buying of county warrants and sentenced to ten years in the penitentiary. The Court spoke of him as a 'man of wealth, power and influence, a merchant of many years. . . .' He was pardoned by Governor Conrad M. Zulick (1885–1889) after two years imprisonment" (30 n).

Benjamin Thomas to S. A. Bentley, 30 August 1881, Copies of Miscellaneous Letters Sent, Pueblo Indian Agency, Denver Federal Records Center, reports that Barth was back at Zuni in that year. The "notorious rascal" took Zuni horses and failed to pay for them.

277. *Annual Report of the Commissioner of Indian Affairs, 1871,* 590; F. M. Pullman to Pedro Pino, 15 May 1870, MS.6.PP.1.37, Cushing Collection, SWM.

278. *Santa Fe Weekly New Mexican,* 11 February 1873, reported "a rumor has reached Prescott of a fight between Indians of Zuni and Navajos on the Rio Puerco Azul, in which 39 Navajos and 15 Indians of Zuni were killed" (p. 2, col. 1).

279. A plate of the photo in Frank McNitt, *Navajo Wars: Military Campaigns, Slave Raids and Reprisals* (Albuquerque: University of New Mexico Press, 1972) identifies the photographer as William Henry Jackson, but James D. Horan, *Timothy O'Sullivan: America's Forgotten Photographer* (New York: Bonanza Books, 1966), 297–99, correctly points out that O'Sullivan was Wheeler's photographer at Zuni.

280. Francis Klett, "The Zuni Indians of New Mexico," *Popular Science Monthly* 5 (May to October 1874): 580–87. Klett, like a number of others during his era, believed the Pueblo Indians in general and the Zunis in particular were descended from the Aztecs. This theory has been dismissed by experts. Scientists believe that the Zunis descended from the Hohokom, Mogollon, and Anasazi peoples. When Klett spoke of the *cacique,* on several occasions his description seemed to indicate that Pino was referring instead to the *bekwinne* or sun priest.

281. Ibid.

282. Ibid.

283. Ibid.

284. Ibid.

285. Ibid.; Francis Klett, "The Cochina: A Dance at the Pueblo of Zuni," in *Report upon United States Geographical Surveys West of the One Hundredth Meridian*, vol. 7, *Archaeology* (Washington, D.C.: GPO, 1875–1889), 332–36. This report suggests Klett may have seen more than one dance. Both of these articles by Klett were likely ones which Cushing may have seen; they may have influenced his and Powell's decision for Cushing to go to the pueblo.

286. Francis Klett to Pedro Pino, 23 July 1873, MS.6.PP.1.25, Cushing Collection, SWM.

287. George M. Wheeler, *Report upon United States Geographical Surveys West of the One Hundredth Meridian*, vol. 1. *Geographical* (Washington, D.C.: U.S. Geological Survey, 1889), 61.

288. George M. Wheeler to Pedro Pino, 1 September 1873, MS.6.PP.1.42, Cushing Collection, SWM.

289. Wheeler, 222.

290. George M. Wheeler, *Report upon United States Geographical Surveys West of the One Hundredth Meridian*, 7 vols. (Washington, D.C.: U.S. Geological Survey, 1875–1889), appendix LL, 135.

291. Fred Myers to Pedro Pino, 19 November 1873, MS.6.PP.1.29, Cushing Collection, SWM.

Chapter 8

292. *Annual Report of the Secretary of the Interior, 1869–1870*, 41st Cong., 2d sess., 693; *Annual Report of the Commissioner of Indian Affairs, 1871* (Washington, D.C.: GPO, 1872), 391.

293. Ben Thomas to William Burgess, 7 December 1874, Copies of Miscellaneous Letters Sent, Pueblo Indian Agency, 12/1/74–2/12/76, Record Group 75, Denver Federal Records Center.

294. Ben Thomas to William Wallace, 7 December 1874, Copies of Miscellaneous Letters Sent, Pueblo Indian Agency, 12/l/74–2/12/76, Record Group 75, Denver Federal Records Center.

295. Ben Thomas to William Burgess, 3 March 1875, Copies of Miscellaneous Letters Sent, Pueblo Indian Agency, 12/l/74–2/12/76, Record Group 75, Denver Federal Records Center, emphasis in original.

296. Nutria villages, Pescado, and Ojo Caliente.

297. *Annual Report of the Secretary of the Interior, 1875*, 44th Cong., lst sess., H. Doc., 586, emphasis added.

298. *Santa Fe Weekly New Mexican*, 26 January 1875, p. 1, col. 4; Ben Thomas to Gobernador del Pueblo de Zuni, 14 June 1875, MS.6.PP.1.41, Cushing Collection, SWM; Charles P. Eagan,

Quartermaster to Pedro Pino, 22 April 1875, MS.6.PP.1.16, Cushing Collection, SWM.

299. *Santa Fe Weekly New Mexican*, 5 October 1875.

300. Juan Christobal Armijo to Pedro Pino, August 1875 and [?] 1875, MS.6.PP.1.1, Cushing Collection, SWM.

301. Ben Thomas to Alcalde Juero, 13 July 1875, Copies of Miscellaneous Letters Sent, Pueblo Indian Agency, 12/l/74–2/ 12/76, Record Group 75, Denver Federal Records Center.

302. The "grant" was from the Spanish and not the Mexican government, though Pino always claimed a grant from the Mexican government. Thomas should already have seen the grant since it was deposited with him in the first place, and he had personally deposited it with the surveyor general.

303. Ben Thomas to Pedro Pino, 20 April 1876, Copies of Miscellaneous Letters Sent, Pueblo Indian Agency, 2/12/76–6/ 18/77, Record Group 75, Denver Federal Records Center, emphasis added.

304. Ben Thomas to Commissioner of Indian Affairs, 28 February 1877, Copies of Miscellaneous Letters Sent, Pueblo Indian Agency, 2/12/76–6/18/77, Record Group 75, Denver Federal Records Center.

305. H. C. Hodge to Pedro Pino, 1 July 1875, MS.6.PP.1.23, Cushing Collection, SWM.

306. R. H. Smith, "Among the Zunis," parts 1 and 2, *Juvenile Instructor* 11 (11 September 1876): 202 and (1 October 1876): 223–24; Ammon Tenney, "Journal of Ammon Tenney," manuscript, 20 October 1875 to 10 September 1876, LDS Church Archives, Salt Lake City. During the next two months, the Mormons reported that they baptized 111 Zunis. Among them were "Jun [Juan] Bautista" and probably Ramon Luna. Charles S. Peterson, *Take Up Your Mission: Mormon Colonizing along the Little Colorado River, 1870–1900* (Tucson: University of Arizona Press, 1973), 204–05.

307. Smith, 202, 223–24.

308. Tenney. This is one description which sounds as though it was recorded verbatim from Pedro Pino and not abbreviated. In a personal conversation with the author, Myra Ellen Jenkins, curator of the New Mexico State Archives, reported that similar complaints were voiced by other pueblos. In the meantime, the Navajos had swelled with success and begun to claim more and more territory In an 1876 council, Navajos claimed all of Zuni

and Hopi territory and wished to go to Washington to ask for even more land *(Navajo Calendar,* 6 April 1876 [n.p., n.d.]).

309. Peterson reported Woodruff's interest and the founding of St. Johns, 204-5.

310. Irving Telling, "History of Ramah, New Mexico," manuscript, 1939, p. 3, E. Richard Hart Papers, Marriott Library, University of Utah, Salt Lake City.

311. H. L[lewelyn]. H[arris]., "A Wonderful Manifestation," *The Millennial Star* 41 (2 June 1879): 337–41.

312. Ibid.; James H. Simpson, *Journal of a Military Reconnaissance from Santa Fe New Mexico to the Navajo Country Made in 1849,* edited and annotated by Frank McNitt (Norman: University of Oklahoma Press, 1964), 126 n; Irving Telling, "Ramah, New Mexico, 1876–1900: An Historical Episode with Some Value Analysis," *Utah State Historical Society Quarterly* 21, no. 2 (April 1953): 119; Hubert Howe Bancroft, *History of Arizona and New Mexico* (San Francisco: The History Company Publishers, 1889), 740.

313. Sylvester Baxter, "The Father of the Pueblos," *Harpers's New Monthly Magazine,* June 1882, 72.

314. S. Lyman Tyler, *A History of Indian Policy* (Washington, D.C.: Bureau of Indian Affairs, 1973), 94.

315. Thomas to Assistant Adjutant Generals, 1 December 1876, Copies of Miscellaneous Letters Sent, Pueblo Indian Agency, 2/12/76–6/18/77, RG 75, Denver Federal Records Center.

316. *Annual Report of the Department of the Interior, 1876–1877,* 44th. Cong., 1st. sess., 1876, H. Doc., Serial Set 1749, 515.

317. Ben Thomas to Commissioner of Indian Affairs, 28 February 1877, Copies of Miscellaneous Letters Sent, Pueblo Indian Agency, 2/12/76–6/18/77, RG 75, Denver Federal Records Center.

Chapter 9

318. Ben Thomas to J. O. Smith, 28 February 1877, Copies of Miscellaneous Letters Sent, Pueblo Indian Agency, 2/12/76–6/18/77, RG 75, Denver Federal Records Center (hereafter cited as CMLS, PIA, RG 75, DFRC). Throughout the next decade, many troubles developed for the Zunis because of the vague wording of the description Thomas submitted, but eventually, with Cushing's help later, the Zunis were able to at least maintain control over their three main farming villages.

319. The Zuni River. Thomas is correct in stating that Nutrias, Pescado, and Ojo Caliente were the main farming villages, but

he underestimates how far the Zunis ranged to plant in other areas. Zunis farmed as far away as the present site of Houck, and St. Johns, Arizona.

320. Thomas to Smith, 28 February 1877.

321. Ben Thomas to Pedro Pino, February 1877, CMLS, PIA, 2/12/76–6/18/77, RG 75, DFRC.

322. Ben Thomas to James W. Bennett, 5 February 1877, CMLS, PIA, 2/12/76–6/18/77, RG 75, DFRC; Ben Thomas to E. A. Hoyt, 17 November 1877, CMLS, PIA, RG 75, DFRC; Ben Thomas to Burgess Brothers, Navajo Springs, September 1877, CMLS, PIA, RG 75, DFRC.

323. Ben Thomas to Governor of Zuni, 27 June 1877, CMLS, PIA, RG 75, DFRC.

324. Ben Thomas to Rev. Sheldon Jackson, 2 July 1877; Ben Thomas to H. K. Palmer, 2 July 1877; Ben Thomas to H. K. Palmer, 2 October 1877; all part of CMLS, PIA, RG 75, DFRC.

325. Ben Thomas to Governor of Zuni, August 20, 1877; Ben Thomas to the Governor and Principales of Zuni, 15 February 1878; both part of CMLS, PIA, RG 75, DFRC.

326. Ben Thomas to H. K. Palmer, 15 February 1878, CMLS, PIA, RG 75, DFRC, reports that Palmer made some effort to innoculate the Zunis before vacating the Pueblo; Ben Thomas to H. K. Palmer, 11 March 1878, CMLS, PIA, RG 75, DFRC; "Medical History of Post Ft. Wingate, New Mexico," Records of the Adjutant General's Office, RG 94, vol. 820, p. 70, National Archives.

327. Ben Thomas to Santiago Baca, 1878; Ben Thomas to Auguste Lacome, 20 March 1878; Ben Thomas to Santiago Baca, 17 June 1878; all part of CMLS, PIA, RG 75, DFRC; Ben Thomas to Governor of Zuni (copy of letter from Baca in Spanish), June 1878, MS.6.PP.1.41, Cushing Collection, SWM.

328. Thomas to H. K. Palmer, 20 May 1878, CMLS, PIA, RG 75, DFRC; *Annual Report of the Secretary of the Interior, 1878*, 45th Cong., 3rd sess., H. Doc., Serial Set 1850, 606; Ben Thomas to Governor Pedro Pino and All the Principales of Zuni, 4 September 1878, CMLS, PIA, RG 75, DFRC.

329. Robert G. Athearn, *William Tecumseh Sherman and the Settlement of the West* (Norman: University of Oklahoma Press, 1956, 329–30.

330. Ben Thomas to the Governor of Zuni, Pedro Pino, and All Officers, 30 August 1878, CMLS, PIA, RG 75, DFRC.

331. W. T. Sherman to Pedro Pino, 10 September 1878, MS.6.PP.1.39, Cushing Collection, SWM.
332. Frank Hamilton Cushing, "Biography of Pedro Pino," handwritten manuscript, n. d., Cushing Collection, SWM.
333. Ibid.
334. Thomas to T. F. Ealy, 29 October 1878, CMLS, PIA, RG 75, DFRC; Ruth R. Ealy, *Water in a Thirsty Land* (Author, 1955). The book is a partial presentation of T. F. Ealy's diaries.
335. Ben Thomas to T. F. Ealy, 14 December 1878; Ben Thomas to Commissioner of Indian Affairs, 15 January 1879; Ben Thomas to Patricio Pino, Governor of Zuni, 28 January 1879; T. F. Ealy to Ben Thomas, 25 March 1879, April 1879, and 17 April 1879; Ben Thomas to T. F. Ealy, 26 April 1879; all part of CMLS, PIA, RG 75, DFRC.
336. Ben Thomas to Galen Eastman, 18 July 1879; Ben Thomas to Barnes, 16 May 1879; Ben Thomas to T. F. Ealy, 18 July 1879; all part of CMLS, PIA, RG 75, DFRC. T. F. Ealy to Ben Thomas, 23 May 1879, and T. F. Ealy to Ben Thomas (for Pedro Pino), 22 May 1879, MS.6.PP.1.17, Cushing Collection, SWM.
337. Thomas to Ealy, 18 July 1879.
338. Ferdinand Andrews, "The Indians of New Mexico and Arizona," manuscript, nd, pp. 82–83, Huntington Library, Pasadena, California.
339. Frank Hamilton Cushing, *Zuni Breadstuff,* Indian Notes and Monographs, vol. 8 (1920; reprint, New York: Heye Foundation, Museum of the American Indian, 1974). In the introduction, Frederick J. Dockstader comments on Cushing's place in the field of ethnology (5).
340. Frank H. Cushing, *My Adventures in Zuni,* (Palmer Lake, Colo.: Filter Press, 1967; reprinted from *Century Magazine,* 1882–1883; also the edition edited by Everett L. DeGolyer and published by Peripatetic Press in 1941); Ealy, *Water in a Thirsty Land.*
      Additional information about Cushing's stay in Zuni can be gleaned from numerous sources, many of them previously cited. Of particular note are Clarissa Parsons Fuller, "Frank Hamilton Cushing's Relations to Zuni and the Hemenway Southwestern Expedition; 1879–1889," (master's thesis, University of New Mexico, 1943); Sylvester Baxter, "The Father of the Pueblos," *Harpers's New Monthly Magazine,* June 1882, especially pp. 72–87; Sylvester Baxter, "An Aboriginal Pilgrimage," *Century Magazine,* August 1882, 526–36; letters received from Frank Hamilton

Cushing, 1879–1888, microfilm reel 9, Smithsonian Institution National Anthropological Archives, Washington, D.C.; "Transcript of an interview with F.W. HODGE," manuscript, C-D, 4016, Bancroft Library, Berkeley, California; William E. Curtis, *Children of the Sun* (Chicago: The Inter-Ocean Publishing Co., 1883).

341.   "Zuni, Bureau of Land Management, Santa Fe, N.M.," Pueblo land grant papers, case 5, papers 15–17, New Mexico Archives, Santa Fe. Either Pino hedged about his age, or the information was miscalculated in translation. He claimed he was seventy-five, but Cushing, who was present at this time, clearly indicates that Pino was born in the last decade of the eighteenth century. Pino's deposition includes the following exchange:

> "Question. State your name, age and place of residence.
> Answer. My name is Pedro Pino, my age is Seventy-five years, and I reside, at Zuni in Valencia County Territory of New Mexico.
> Ques. Are you acquainted with the Zuni Pueblo grant, and if so how long have you known it? and where is it [the old pueblo of Zuni] located?
> Ans. I am—since I can remember—on a high mesa south east of the present Indian town of Zuni and distant about three miles.
> Ques. Have you any interest in said grant, and if so, what interest have you?
> Ans. I have, as one of the heirs."

342.   Tilly E. (Matilda Coxe) Stevenson, *Zuni and the Zunians* (Washington, D.C.: n.p., 1881), 24.

343.   "Medical History of Post Fort Wingate New Mexico," microfilm, RG 94, selected papers, Records of the Adjutant General's Office, vol. 820, May 1881, p. 139, National Archives.

344.   Lansing B. Bloom, "Bourke on the Southwest," *New Mexico Historical Review* 12, nos. 1 and 4 (January and October 1937): iii, 117, 188–93; Fuller.

345.   Bloom, 188–93.

346.   Bloom, 189. The term "gens" has been replaced by the more recognizable term "clan."

347.   José Palle is listed as clan captain of Corn Clan, Juan Septimo is "the silver smith" of the Water Clan, and Pedro Pino a captain in the Eagle Clan.

348. Bloom, 191–92. Douglas Dher Graham opened a store to the
south of the pueblo in 1879. He was the most important trader
at Zuni for twenty years and was later appointed agent to the
Pueblo Indians. He is known in oral tradition as Tsibon
K'winna, or "Black Beard."

349. Ben Thomas to T. F. Ealy, 4 June 1881; T. F. Ealy to Ben Thomas,
17 June 1881; both are Register of Letters Received (RLR), PIA,
RG 75, DFRC; *Annual Report of the Department of Interior*, 47th
Cong., lst sess., 1881, H. Doc., Serial Set 2018, 198; Fuller, 60.

350. Fuller, 60; Bloom, 188–93.

351. Fuller, 60; Bloom, 188–93. Washington Matthews, another ethnologist in the area during the period, had descriptions for both
Bentley and Mrs. Stevenson. Bentley was described as "one of
those cadaverous sky-pilots who wear a stereotyped smile on their
faces" (Washington Matthews to Frank Hamilton Cushing, 21
July 1881, MS.6.Zuni.1.39, Cushing Collection, SWM). Matthews
later described Mrs. Stevenson as "that learned authoress and sci-
entistess" (Washington Matthews to Frank Hamilton Cushing, 23
June 1891, MS.6.Zuni.1.69, Cushing Collection, SWM). Bentley
and Stevenson had equally derogatory appraisals of Cushing.

352. Fuller, 63.

353. Ibid., 63–64.

354. Frank Hamilton Cushing to Spencer F. Baird, 4 December
1881, letters received from Frank Hamilton Cushing,
1879–1888, microfilm reel 9, Smithsonian Institution National
Anthropological Archives, Washington, D.C.; Frank Hamilton
Cushing to Ben Thomas, 29 November 1881, RLR, PIA, RG 75,
DFRC reports that he arrested Roman (Ramon) Luna, and
noted "insubordination" and "interference" by Bentley. Samuel
A. Bentley to Ben Thomas, 29 November 1881, RLR, PIA, RG
75, DFRC reports Cushing's "arrest of one of the leading Zuni
Indians" and asks if Cushing has that authority. Ramon Luna
was also known as Mu:ma, W'mu'n, or Mormon, and later
became governor during the years from 1895–1902 (apparently with several breaks in the tenure).

355. Fuller, 61. Elsewhere the story is told of a Zuni who was paid a
dime to be baptized and thus gained the name of "Ten Cent
Mormon" (it is unclear if this is the same "Mormon" as Ramon
Luna). Cushing to Baird, 4 December 1881.

356. Cushing to Baird, 4 December 1881.

357. Ibid. Bourke reported that "for each man killed in war, they [the Zunis] are allowed to wear on wrist four small sea shells. Patricio had on his arm *twenty* of these, corroborating his statement that in years gone by he had made 5 Navajos bite the dust" (Bloom, 243). In *Zuni Breadstuff,* Cushing recounts an incident when Patricio met the relative of a Navajo he had killed and how, incredibly, they traded together.

   In "Pueblo Pages," *The Journal,* 28 February 1882, from a Smithsonian Institution National Anthropological Archives clipping file, Cushing claimed to have taken a Navajo scalp himself, and thus was able to wear the four sea shells, but other indications suggest that Cushing requested and received a musty scalp from the archives of the Smithsonian Institution to satisfy the requirements to join the Priesthood of the Bow.

358. Edward H. Spicer, *Cycles of Conquest* (Tucson: University of Arizona Press, 1962), 199.

359. Oakah L. Jones, Jr., introduction to *My Adventures in Zuni,* viii.

360. Ward Alan Minge, *Acoma: Pueblo in the Sky* (Albuquerque: University of New Mexico Press, 1976), 65.

361. Fuller, 62.

362. Ibid.

363. Frank Hamilton Cushing to Pedro Pino, 28 September 1879, MS.6.PP.1.14, Cushing Collection, SWM.

364. Fuller, 68.

Chapter 10

365. Frank Hamilton Cushing to Spencer F. Baird, 4 December 1881, letters received from Frank Hamilton Cushing, 1879–1888, microfilm reel 9, Smithsonian Institution National Anthropological Archives, Washington, D.C.

366. Frank Hamilton Cushing, "Biography of Pedro Pino," handwritten manuscript, Cushing Collection, SWM.

367. Milburne to Ben Thomas, 19 January 1882, CMLS, PIA, RG 75, DFRC; Ben Thomas to Price, 23 February 1882, enclosing Frank Hamilton Cushing to Ben Thomas, 16 January 1882, letters received, 1881–1907, RG 75, National Archives. Cushing originally intended to take two representative Zuni women along but finally chose a group of only men.

368. Sylvester Baxter, "An Aboriginal Pilgrimage," *Century Magazine,* August 1882, 527.

369. Cushing to Thomas, 16 January 1882.

370. Baxter, 527.
371. Ibid., 526–36.
372. Ibid., 527–28.
373. "Pueblo Pages," *The Journal,* 28 February 1882, from a Smithsonian Institution National Anthropological Archives clipping file.
374. Cushing, "Biography."
375. Cushing, *Zuni Breadstuff,* 541–43.
376. Baxter, 526–36.
377. William E. Curtis, *Children of the Sun* (Chicago: The Inter-Ocean Publishing Co., 1883), 18–19.
378. Curtis, 23.
379. Ibid., 24.
380. John G. Carlisle to Pedro Pino, 5 April 1882, MS.6.PP.1.10, Cushing Collection, SWM.
381. Matilda Coxe Stevenson, "The Zuni Indians,"in *Twenty-third Annual Report of the Bureau of American Ethnology, 1901–1902* (Washington, D.C.: GPO, 1904), 312.
382. Sylvester Baxter, "The Father of the Pueblos," *Harpers's New Monthly Magazine,* June 1882, 86; Curtis, 35.
383. Cushing, *Zuni Breadstuff,* 539–41. Pedro Pino later declined eating anything at Palmer House in Chicago and dined only on food he had packed with him.
384. John A. Logan had been a general in the Civil War and a member of the U.S. House of Representatives (1867–1871), was a member of the U.S. Senate (1871–1877, 1879–1886), and would be a candidate for vice president of the United States in 1884 *(Webster's Biographical Dictionary,* 1970, 913). Teri Schultz, "Bamboozle Me Not at Wounded Knee," *Harper's,* June 1973, 46–56, reports that Logan made the following comment to the Sioux leader, Sitting Bull, "You are fed by the government, clothed by the government, your children are educated by the Government, and all you have and are today is because of the Government. You cannot insult the people of the United States of America or its committees."
385. Documents relating to the Logan affair include the following: "Medical History of Post Fort Wingate, New Mexico" microfilm, RG 94, selected papers, Records of the Adjutant General's Office, vol. 820, May 1881, p. 172, National Archives; Curtis; Frederick Webb Hodge to E. Degolyer, n.d., MS.7.SWM.1.135, Correspondence 1941–1946, Frederick Webb Hodge Manuscript Collection, SWM; Ben Thomas to Hiram Price, 12 April 1883, CMLS, PIA, RG 75, DFRC; *Zuni Indian Reservation in*

New Mexico and Arizona, 48th Cong., 2d sess., December 3, 1883, H. Doc. 11, Serial Set 2296, 7. Baxter was responsible for numerous articles in the press.

386. Charles J. Kappler, *Indian Affairs: Laws and Treaties,* vol. 1, *Laws* (Washington, D.C.: Government Printing Office, 1904), 880.

387. Hodge to Degolyer.

388. "Zuni-Land Zephyrs," *Santa Fe New Mexican Review,* 9 December 1884, p. 4, col. 4.

389. *Santa Fe New Mexican Review,* 6 March 1884, p. 1, col. 1.

390. *Santa Fe New Mexican Review,* 18 June 1884, p.12.

391. "The Nutria Springs Controversy," *Santa Fe Daily New Mexican,* 22 May 1883, p. 2, col. 2.

392. Frank Hamilton Cushing, "The Discovery of Zuni or the Ancient Province of Cibola or the Seven Cities," handwritten manuscript, 1885, Cushing Collection, SWM.

393. Ruth L. Bunzel, "Zuni Origin Myths," in *Forty-seventh Annual Report of the Bureau of American Ethnology, 1929–1930* (Washington, D.C.: GPO, 1932), 585.

394. Ruth L. Bunzel, "Zuni Ritual Poetry," in *Forty-seventh Annual Report of the Bureau of American Ethnology, 1929–1930* (Washington, D.C.: GPO, 1932), 666–67.

395. Frank Hamilton Cushing, *My Adventures in Zuni* (Palmer Lake, Colo.: Filter Press, 1967; reprinted from *Century Magazine,* 1882–1883), 49.

396. Ibid.

Afterword

397. E. Richard Hart, "Zuni Pueblo/U.S. Contact, 1846–1882: Pedro Pino's Diplomatic Struggle" (paper presented at Westward Movements, a conference sponsored by the Canadian Association for American Studies, November 1–3, 1979, Simon Fraser University, Vancouver, Canada).

398. Floyd A. O'Neil and E. Richard Hart, "Fraudulent Land Activities by United States Officials Affecting Title to Zuni Lands," report prepared for the House Committee on Interior and Insular Affairs, 101st Congress, 2d. Session, July 12, 1990.

399. Sandra K. Mathews-Lamb, "Designing and Mischievous Individuals: The Cruzate Grants and the Office of the Surveyor General," *New Mexico Historical Review* 71, no. 4 (October 1996): 344–60.

400. Especially William H. Goetzmann, *Exploration and Empire: The Explorer and the Scientist in the Winning of the American West* (New

York: Alfred A. Knopf, 1971) and *Army Exploration in the American West, 1803–1863* (Lincoln: University of Nebraska Press, 1979).

401. Jesse Green, *Zuni: Selected Writings of Frank Hamilton Cushing* (Lincoln: University of Nebraska Press, 1979) and *Cushing at Zuni: The Correspondence and Journals of Frank Hamilton Cushing, 1879–1984* (Albuquerque: University of New Mexico Press, 1990).

402. Especially David J. Weber, *The Spanish Frontier in North America* (New Haven: Yale University Press, 1992); *The Mexican Frontier, 1821–1846: The American Southwest under Mexico* (Albuquerque: University of New Mexico Press, 1982); and *Richard H. Kern: Expeditionary Artist in the Far Southwest, 1848–1853* (Albuquerque: University of New Mexico Press, 1985).

403. Among John L. Kessel's many important contributions is *Kiva, Cross and Crown: The Pecos Indians and New Mexico, 1540–1840* (Washington, D.C.: National Park Service, 1979).

404. Over the years he has done much outstanding work on Zuni, including T. J. Ferguson, *Historic Zuni Architecture and Society: An Archaeological Application of Space Syntax* (Tucson: University of Arizona Press, 1996).

Appendices

405. Frank Hamilton Cushing, "Biography of Pedro Pino," handwritten manuscript, n.d., Frank Hamilton Cushing Manuscript Collection, Pedro Pino Series, Pedro Pino Biography—Lai-A-Ai-Kai-Luh Folder, MS.6.PP.4.1. Courtesy of the Southwest Museum, Los Angeles, California.

406. Brackets in original. The more common term today is "clan."

407. W. P. Boyakin, "Orders No. 41," Frank Hamilton Cushing Manuscript Collection, Pedro Pino Series, Pedro Pino/H. P. Boyakin Correspondence Folder, MS.6.PP.1.5. Courtesy of the Southwest Museum, Los Angeles, California.

408. "Zuni, Bureau of Land Management, Santa Fe, N.M.," Pueblo land grant papers, case 5, papers 11–14, certified translation of the "original" Spanish grant, 31 December 1878 (grant dated 25 September 1689), New Mexico Archives, Santa Fe.

409. This treaty was signed by the pueblos of Santa Clara, Tesuque, Nambé, Santo Domingo, Jemez, San Felipe, San Ildefonso, Cochiti, Santa Ana, and Zia during the month of July and by Zuni (probably Pedro Pino) in August. Annie Heloise Abel, *The Official Correspondence of James S. Calhoun* (Washington, D.C.: GPO, 1915), 237–46.

Index